PASTORAL THEOLOGY

PASTORAL THEOLOGY

A Black-Church Perspective

JAMES H. HARRIS

Fortress Press/Minneapolis

PASTORAL THEOLOGY
A Black-Church Perspective

Cover design: Terry Bentley

Library of Congress Cataloging-in-Publication Data

Harris, James H., 1952–
    Pastoral theology : A black-church perspective / James H. Harris.
        p.   cm.
    Includes bibliographical references and index.
    ISBN 0-8006-2502-1 (alk. paper)
    1. Afro-American churches.   2. Black theology.   3. Pastoral
theology.   I. Title.
BR563.N4H376   1991
253'.089'96073—dc20   91-13457
                                                                              CIP

The paper used in this publication meets the minimum requirements of American National Standard for Information Sciences—Permanence of Paper for Printed Library Materials, ANSI Z329.48-1984.   ∞™

Manufactured in the U.S.A.   AF 1-2502
95   94   93   92   91   1   2   3   4   5   6   7   8   9   10

To the memories of my dear mother and father,
Carrie Anna Harris and Richard Harris,
and to those who
love and support the black church

Contents

Preface

Pastoral theology is liberation theology because it is grounded in praxis. Its focus is comprehensive and specific. It deals with developing and implementing policies and programs in the church and community that convey the meaning of Christianity in practical life situations. It is the understanding of God and the world that governs the life and work of the pastor and parishioners. Being a pastor is a calling! It requires an inordinate amount of love and sacrifice because the work of the pastor is often thankless and extremely demanding. It is also a constant struggle that involves motivation, change, continuity, teaching, preaching, counseling, managing, and a host of other skills, emotions, and activities. The pastor is both admired and hated, trusted and distrusted, supported and repudiated. The pastor is both prophet and politician—balancing life and work between theory and practice. He or she must have a vision of ministry and a plan for accomplishing that vision through the people who constitute the church and community. Ideas, hopes, dreams, and plans of the pastor need to become the ideas and dreams of the people. Church people have to take part in their own Christian growth, and every pastor has stories of the greatest ideas, programs, and plans that have failed because the people did not support the dream or participate in the process of developing and implementing the vision for the church.

The pastor has to have a vicarious view of the church and ministry—placing himself or herself in the position of others as Jesus often did. Moreover, she or he needs to develop a basic approach to ministry and master the techniques of pastoral ministry with boldness. "The Spirit that God has given us does not make us timid; instead, his Spirit fills us with power, love, and self-control" (2 Tim. 1:7).

My colleagues in the ministry and academia have been very faithful in helping to shape and mold my thoughts on the black church and its role in the liberation struggle. My professors in pastoral theology and ministry, Allix B. James, Miles Jones, Samuel M. Carter, and the late Paul Nichols were all mentors. Dr. Samuel DeWitt Proctor, Dr. Harold E. Braxton and Dr. Wallace J. Cook have taught me a great deal about the pastor's work, and I am grateful to each of them. I am also indebted to Vanessa Harris Bond, Ruth Allmond, and the following pastors—Geoffrey Guns, Lorenzo York, G. Vincent Lewis, Douglas Harris, Robert L. Stephens, Jerome Ross, Robert Murray, and Elliott Cuff—who read the manuscript during different stages of its development and offered valuable yet critical assessments of my thoughts. King E. Davis read parts of the manuscript and was extremely helpful in his advice and evaluation of it. Martha Ryan, Stanley Osborne, Demetrius Alexander, and Kelvin Fowler assisted in several important ways throughout the development of the manuscript. Charles F. Abel has encouraged and helped me in this project as he did in my earlier work. Lewis V. Baldwin read the complete manuscript and offered valuable suggestions for improvement; I am indebted to him for his help.

Some parts of this manuscript have been presented in one form or another to Mount Pleasant Baptist Church, Norfolk, Virginia, and Second Baptist Church in Richmond, Virginia, and to academic groups, including senior and graduate students at Old Dominion University who were in my Seminar on Liberation Philosophy and hundreds of ministers and laypersons in the Evans-Smith Institute for Black Church Studies, a continuing education program where I taught for nearly ten years. I also extend special thanks to three special secretaries, Janet D. Tard, Crystal Hawkins, and Evangeline Ann White, who learned that when it comes to typing manuscripts, "there is nothing permanent except change" (Heraclitus 540–480 B.C.E.). The typing and proofreading skills of Mrs. Evangeline Buggs and Mrs. Dora Newman helped to meet the demands of a hectic schedule.

I am very grateful to the following pastors or their staffs who provided valuable information about their churches: Dr. Charles Booth, the Reverend Thomas E. Smith, Dr. Wyatt Tee Walker, and Dr. John H. Corbitt.

A special word of thanks is extended to the late Dr. Paul Nichols, a pastor and Dean of the School of Theology, Virginia Union University, and Mrs. Gloria Taylor, a doctoral candidate at the Presbyterian School of Christian Education and formerly the Director of the Joseph Nash Multicultural Resource Collection of the Ecumenical Resource Center in Richmond, Virginia. They offered valuable suggestions regarding chapter six, "Christian Education."

Finally, I am most indebted to the distinguished professor Gayraud Wilmore, now at the Interdenominational Theological Center in Atlanta. Dr.

Wilmore agreed to midwife this project during a time that he was extremely busy. His critical reading and lengthy discussions of the manuscript have had a profound influence upon my understanding of the church and black theology. Without his help, this project would not be in its present form. To him, I am eternally grateful.

My wife, Demetrius, and my sons, James Corey and Cameron, are my source of inspiration. I am always thankful for their willingness to share me with so many people in the church and community.

PART ONE
The Black Church

1

Blacks, Evangelicalism, and Beyond

The preaching of the gospel that does not focus on the oppressed is anti-evangelical.
—Gayraud Wilmore

Are the people of God truly God's people if they oppress the poor? Is the church really the church if it does not work to free the oppressed?
—Ronald J. Sider

God did not send the Son into the world to condemn the world, but in order that the world might be saved through him.
—John 3:17

Historically, evangelistic fervor by preachers and laypersons, blacks and whites, has not altered the social structure in a manner that favors the poor and oppressed. From slavery to the Civil Rights movement, the church has played an indecisive and somewhat passive role in changing the status quo. It has vacillated between vocal protest and pious acquiescence, between radical confrontation and diplomatic compromise. Carter G. Woodson, in describing the historical black church, says that it has been "a sort of balance wheel,"[1] that is, weighing public opinion before taking a radical position. He goes on to say, "This conservatism has no doubt saved the Negro from the fate of other oppressed groups who have suffered extermination because of the failure to handle their case more diplomatically."[2] While the preacher and the church have struggled to retain theological integrity without being coopted politically, the effort has often resulted in ambivalence and paradox. The church has appeared to be tepid on issues of liberation by separating the liberation motif from the essence of evangelism. However, true evangelical Christianity is liberative and transformative.[3] The time has come, however, for the black church, as the largest and most significant institution

3

in the life of black Americans, to be the leader in fostering liberation and social change.

The church needs to do more than what most modern evangelicals typically do—praising God and winning souls to Jesus Christ through focusing on personal salvation and a "Praise the Lord . . . Thank you Jesus" mentality that concentrates on salvation from personal sin—because such a focus overlooks oppression, injustice, poverty, and a host of other social ills as manifestations of sinfulness. This is why Jerry Falwell and other evangelicals like him could visit South Africa and return to the United States without condemning apartheid as the evil and oppressive force that it is. This colonial mentality, supported by prevailing conservative evangelical theology and politics, is virtually unconcerned about black people as victims of racism and injustice. Evangelism as "good news" means that the church cannot give lip service to concerns about social evils while preaching that Americans are God's chosen people because this ignores blacks who have borne the burden of social and political persecution by those who claim to be interested in the social dimension of the gospel and because this supports the political, classist, and economic status quo.

Moreover, the black church has fallen short in its commitment to liberation and social change, reflecting the conservatism of the modern white evangelical movement. In confronting this issue as it relates to black Christians, James Cone says:

> Without a clearly articulated theological position in creeds and theological text books, black preachers and their members have nowhere else to turn for theological knowledge and spiritual renewal except conservative, white, evangelical churches. Of course, some black preachers and lay persons can and do transcend white theology and spirituality, but unfortunately, most do not know how to distinguish between black faith and white religion. And with the appearance of electronic church (on radio and television), black Christians are being lured from their spiritual heritage in black churches to the false gods of the Jerry Falwells of this world. Without a critical black theology . . . black preachers are left with the option of simply imitating the false gods of the electronic church in order to keep their congregations from deserting the 11:00 A.M. service and other activities of their churches.[4]

The religion of the black church, although historically different in expression, needs to be radically different in its ability to foster a transformation of the condition of black urban life. This means that the black preacher has a responsibility to reexamine the gospel message in light of the enigmatic social reality that constantly stares blacks and the poor in the face. The preaching, prayers, program activities, and everything else the church does in the name of the gospel of Jesus Christ need to reflect the belief that Jesus was and is the liberator as black theology (and particularly James Cone) has always maintained. Encouraging people to accept Jesus, which is a major focus of evangelism, should also mean enabling them to become whole persons who are free and equal, no longer gripped by the awesome, yet empty hand of poverty and oppression. Freedom and equality under God are not abstract philosophical constructs as rationalism, empiricism, or Platonic idealism are. Justice, freedom, and equality are embedded in Christian faith and biblical tradition—something that the strands of evangelicalism seem to ignore.

Understanding Modern Evangelicalism

Evangelicalism is a multifaceted movement by various leaders and subcultures with roots in the history, beliefs, and practices of Christian orthodoxy. Ronald Nash, in his book *Evangelicals in America*, says, "After the Protestant Reformation in the sixteenth century, the word 'evangelical' was used by certain groups of Protestants to distinguish themselves from Roman Catholics who championed sacramental salvation."[5] Later, especially during the eighteenth century, evangelicalism took on an additional meaning. The word was used to describe the revivals that swept through the American colonies.[6]

Evangelicalism in the United States is a complex and variegated mosaic of Fundamentalism, Pentecostalism, and the evangelical mainstream. Although these groups have significant differences, they all believe in personal salvation. "All three groups hold that conversion is a definite, decisive, and profoundly life-changing experience."[7] Historically, evangelicalism has been divided and ambivalent on the issue of relating the gospel to liberation. However, contemporary evangelicalism is lopsidedly conservative in its interpretation of Scripture and its political activism. In addition, the belief in *Sola Scriptura* fails to acknowledge that the Scripture overwhelmingly supports the position of liberation theology regarding God taking sides with the poor and oppressed rather than with rich oppressors.

The complexity of evangelicalism defies a simple description because some denominations have both evangelical and mainline constituents. For example, the United Presbyterian Church is thought to be mainline while the Presbyterian Church of America is perceived as evangelical. The American Lutheran Church, a mainline denomination, merged in 1988 with the Lutheran Church of America and the Association of Evangelical Lutheran Churches to form the Evangelical Lutheran Church in America. There are also evangelicals within Catholicism.

Some radical nineteenth-century evangelicals, such as Jonathan Blanchard, the founder of Wheaton College, and Charles G. Finney, reformer, abolitionist, revivalist, and president of Oberlin College, have stood on the side of the poor and the oppressed in their fight against slavery. In the same way as William Lloyd Garrison, these men, along with Theodore Weld, a Finney disciple, devoted their lives to a gospel that demanded personal salvation and social reform.[8] Theodore Weld was absorbed in the antislavery struggle of the 1830s. Donald Dayton says, "Weld's identification with the black community was profound and belies the common accusation that abolitionists were nonetheless racially prejudiced."[9]

The history of the evangelical movement suggests that there has been no absolute dichotomy between religion and politics in the sense that some conservatives would have us believe. Inasmuch as slavery has been the most degrading and controversial social, political, and moral problem to face modern society, the evangelicals who fought against it were clearly more committed to a just and egalitarian society than the modern evangelicals who fail to speak against apartheid in South Africa or racial and economic injustice in the United States. Richard John Neuhaus, in his book *The Naked Public Square*, suggests that the struggle in the United States for independence and the abolition of slavery has roots in American revivalism. He writes:

> Historians have argued that the roots of America's struggle for independence from Britain are to be found in the Great Awakening, the religious revival of the eighteenth century. A hundred years later, the movement for the abolition of slavery was empowered, and often resisted, by religious forces. This century's prohibition of alcoholic drink was motored by evangelical Protestants. . . . In those days, indeed until very recently, all Protestants called themselves "evangelical."[10]

While evangelicals are now described differently from some other mainline religious groups because of their beliefs and political practices, Neuhaus further describes evangelicalism:

> To be evangelical meant simply that one was not Roman Catholic. . . . The term "evangelical" was withdrawn from circulation for a time, only to come back in the 1950s as the polite word for fundamentalist. . . . "Evangelical" is a full-blooded word, beside which "liberal" and "mainline" look anemic. "Liberal" speaks of tolerance and "mainline" is a synonym for conventional. . . . "Evangelical" signals a position that is gospel based and inspired. . . . Some of the more bellicose political activists today are so self-confident that they no longer feel the need to disguise their convictions by the polite terminology. They come right out and call themselves fundamentalists.[11]

Fundamentalism, then, is a major component of the modern evangelical movement, and its most well-known adherent, Jerry Falwell, is also one of the leading conservative social activists of modern times. Some intellectual and academic evangelicals include Donald Bloesch, Jefferson Davis, and Carl F. H. Henry. Concerning intellectuals and evangelicalism, Nash says:

> While Carl F. H. Henry's name is not nearly so familiar to the general public as that of Billy Graham or Jerry Falwell, he has probably had more influence on the development of Contemporary Evangelicalism than anyone, save Graham. Without question, Carl Henry is the foremost evangelical theologian of the twentieth century.[12]

Post–World War II evangelicals such as Billy Graham, Jerry Falwell, Oral Roberts, Charles Colson, Robert Schuller, and their cohorts seem to associate with the middle class and the rich. A few others, more in the tradition of pre–Civil War activists like Finney and Weld, are concentrating on liberating people from poverty and injustice. Ronald J. Sider, in his article "An Evangelical Theology of Liberation," questions the hermeneutical soundness of evangelical theology that fails to consider the liberation themes found throughout the Bible. He writes in connection with the Bible's emphasis on the poor and oppressed:

> In light of this clear biblical teaching, how biblical is our evangelical theology? Certainly there have been some great moments of faithfulness. Wesley, Wilberforce, and Charles Finney's evangelical abolitionists stood solidly in the biblical tradition in their search for justice for the poor and oppressed of their time. But twentieth-century evangelicals have not by and large followed their example. I think we must confess that the evangelical community is largely on the side of the rich oppressors rather than the oppressed poor.[13]

On the question of liberation, Ronald Sider argues that evangelical theology has been unbiblical and heretical because it has essentially ignored the biblical teaching that God is on the side of the poor while insisting on belief in the sole authority of Scripture. The conservative evangelicals who ignore the radical message of the prophets and Jesus Christ have done a disservice to the Bible and the people of God. They have also abandoned much of the historical role that evangelicals have played in addressing social and political issues that concern the poor and oppressed.

J. Lawrence Burkholder, in an appraisal of popular evangelicalism, explains the difference between traditional evangelicalism and post–World War II evangelicals.

> Historically Evangelicals have been non-conformists. Their roots are sectarian and their social position has until recent times reinforced non-conformist attitudes. But, with post–World War II upward mobility, their social position has made them participants in the American dream. This has meant that their relationship to culture has changed fundamentally, and the content of their social criticism has changed accordingly. Whereas their earlier attitudes emanated from the consciousness of the dispossessed and were directed against the powerful . . . now they are directed against those who would threaten the establishment.[14]

Inasmuch as blacks are outside of the establishment circle, that is, on the periphery, we cannot afford to be lured into the popular evangelical mode of theology and ministry. However, Third World Christians, black liberation pastors and theologians, and others who are committed to liberation and change can begin to dialogue with those evangelicals who advocate social justice as a biblical imperative. As radical evangelicals try to understand their faith in relationship to the social structure, black liberationists can seize this opening as an opportunity to work together. In this connection, Wes Michaelson, in his article "Evangelicalism and Radical Discipleship," makes an interesting point.

> Those who have emerged from evangelical backgrounds to a faith which refuses to segregate personal conversion and social activism find a sense of rapport with these Christians. From them we hear clear words of judgment about the American economic order and its worldwide dominion over people's lives—words which are prompted by the biblical message, but which have been foreign to evangelical conversation.[15]

This truth rings loudly in the ears of some black churchgoers while others are influenced by the more conservative preachers who dominate the airwaves in the United States and the Third World. For example, Jimmy Swaggart, Jerry Falwell, Billy Graham, and others advocate conforming to their conservative biblical and political ideology while essentially denying the radical implications of the gospel. They essentially deal with Americanism, capitalism, and racism. Moreover, they believe that poor people are responsible for their own poverty, government has already done too much for blacks, and the present social order is too liberal.

Modern conservative evangelicalism emphasizes the moral value of maintaining and perpetuating the status quo rather than demanding that extant cultural, social, and political practices and institutions be transformed. The sermons, writings, and other forms of propaganda advocated by evangelicals have major political implications for those who subsist at the bottom of the social and economic pecking order, and whose lives require the transformation of the social system and its rules. The modern evangelical movement seeks to obviate the Civil Rights movement and its philosophy of liberation and social change. However, this current practice does not coincide with the gospel message and its example of freedom and liberation for the individual and society.

Radical Evangelicalism:
The Soweto Model

One of the most refreshingly new and powerful statements on evangelicalism has come from a group in Soweto called the "Concerned Evangelicals." Their publication entitled *Evangelical Witness in South Africa* reflects the sentiment of the oppressed. South Africa's evangelical community is crying for justice in the same sense as the prophet Amos: "Let justice roll down like waters, and righteousness like an everflowing stream" (Amos 5:24). Their cry is a powerful statement that gives substance to evangelicalism. What is the theological position of the fundamentalist on race and gender oppression? The framers of this document boldly assert their belief that "salvation and social change cannot be separated from one another."[16] While salvation is a necessary, critical, and important development in Christian nurture, it cannot be individualistic, that is, ending with the experience of spiritual ecstacy. Too often this posture has characterized the evangelical community. Unsuspecting Christians have been lured into the status quo nature of society, conforming to popular opinion and conservative values. However, the Concerned Evangelicals of Soweto inform us that

> born again Christians must always be dissatisfied about the world and with existing social orders or systems. They must not be static but they must be dynamic in the direction of radical change. We believe that God, through Jesus Christ, is calling us to salvation, to a radical change of the structures of society. We believe that we are called to effect these changes. To us it is not a matter of what political system or party is involved, but it is a question of how just the system is and how compatible it is with the gospel.[17]

Clearly, there is no justice in apartheid, and as a political system it is grossly incompatible with the gospel. Nevertheless, evangelicals in the United States and other places have supported the system. According to some of the radical evangelicals, the church is in complicity with the prevailing social structure. It acquiesces rather than forces change. They state the point more emphatically: "There is a general tendency of the church to conform to the norms of the values of the society of its time even when they are at variance with the gospel of the Lord Jesus Christ. The evangelical tradition excels in this regard."[18]

For blacks in the United States and throughout the world, *Evangelical Witness in South Africa* provides the necessary model of self-criticism and evaluation to help transform the church from its role as participant in the status quo to one that confronts and endeavors to change the system.

The black church needs to become outraged at the circumstances of blacks at home and abroad. When this rage is turned into action, the church will cease to be taken for granted. It will no longer be perceived as an ally of the oppressor, but a prophetic voice and meaningful agent of liberation and change.

Christology and Transformation

In reading the Synoptic Gospels and the Gospel of John, we see a Christ who transforms the prevailing perceptions and practices of that day, one whose messages and life-style did not conform to the wishes of the Pharisees and scribes or any religious leaders, groups, or sects. In this sense, Jesus would not have been part of an evangelical movement that places a priority on acceptance of the status quo. And, for blacks, the status quo needs to be changed because it facilitates oppression rather than liberation. That is precisely why James Cone is correct when he writes: "There is no liberation without transformation, that is, without the struggle for freedom in this world. There is no liberation without the commitment of revolutionary action against injustice, slavery, and oppression."[19]

Likewise, the apostle Paul embraces the spirit of Christ in writing to the church at Rome: "Do not be conformed to this world, but be transformed by the renewing of your minds, so that you may discern what is the will of God—what is good and acceptable and perfect" (Rom. 12:2). Paul understood what it meant to be transformed because of his own personal experience with Christ. However, he sought to proclaim the gospel of transformation to the churches from Tarsus to Rome. St. Augustine understood transformation, too. He is probably the best example the Middle Ages have to offer for the transforming power of Christ. In his *Confessions*, he explains how he came to accept Jesus Christ and to abide by his will. For Augustine, Jesus Christ is the transformer of culture.[20] Today there is a growing need for Christ to reign, rather than the Christian church which has, to some extent, become perverted and corrupt. There is indeed a difference between Jesus Christ and Christianity, and if the focus of evangelism is to admonish persons to be like Christ, then that means Christians should have a new worldview because they are new creatures, that is, born again. This is precisely what Jesus demanded in his teachings—that a new outlook be understood, accepted, and practiced.

Jesus Christ is the archetype of freedom: "If you continue in my word . . . the truth will make you free" (John 8:31-32). As the embodiment of these ideals, Jesus concretizes truth and freedom: "I am the way, and the truth, and the life" (John 14:6). God is free to demonstrate what it means to suffer and be in bondage as well as what it means to be free by sending Jesus into the world so that the world might be saved (cf. Phil. 2:5ff.). Ernst Käseman has indicated that the entire New Testament is concerned with the cause of Christian freedom. Indeed, he says that "Jesus means freedom."

Now, what do white evangelicals mean when they say that Jesus will set you free? What is their understanding of freedom? We believe that they mean essentially that Jesus will free one from the grips of personal sin such as drunkenness, lust, or envy. However, when the black preacher in the tradition of black experiential religion says that Jesus will set you free, he or she is talking about freedom not simply from the catalogue of sins to which white evangelicals and fundamentalists so often refer. The black preacher also means freedom from oppression and injustice.

The danger of the evangelical message as espoused by many prominent televangelists from Billy Graham to Jim Bakker is that is does not address the serious ethical problem of social, political, and economic injustice as it pertains to blacks in the urban centers of America. This prompts us to ask: What kind of Aristotelian happiness can black people have while living in the "shadow of death" because of poverty, joblessness, discrimination, and the subtleties of racism? How can it be right or good for a people to be so obviously the victims of an oppressive social, political, and economic order? The Christian church must be about freedom and justice if it is to be about the Word of God.

The prophet Amos became very upset and prophesied against the people of God precisely because of their apathy regarding the poor and others in their midst who were suffering and in need while the Israelites languished in their rituals and form. The church is called to deal with moral questions so that it and society will be transformed, not in order to fit into the prevailing social and political milieu. The prophet is clearly concerned with the absence of justice and righteousness. Worship apart from fairness and goodness is a meaningless exercise in futility that can hardly please God.

> Seek good and not evil, that you may live: and so the Lord, the God of Hosts, shall be with you, just as you have said. . . . Take away from me the noise of your songs; I will not listen to the melody of your harps. But let justice roll down like waters, and righteousness like an everflowing stream." (Amos 5:14, 23-24)

The church does what is biblically and morally right by allowing God's word to speak to the conditions of society. It cannot afford to be an isolated institution, operating as if the world is at peace and God's children are all doing well. It must have an integrated approach to the practice of ministry in an urban environment. Clearly a church that believes in God and in God's power to change the world must also believe in justice and equality not just for whites in the Jeffersonian and utilitarian tradition, but for blacks and other minorities as well. The biblical mandate embedded in the Law and the Prophets as well as the gospel of Jesus Christ requires economic and social change as a concomitant to personal change, brought about by understanding the total scriptural message. In other words, true evangelism is transformational in the sense that one is not only "born anew" spiritually, but that this rebirth should foster a change in one's approach to the prevailing social and political inequities that are endemic in our society. (To be born again, or to be saved, is to be redeemed or liberated not only from sin and guilt, but also from oppression and injustice.)

The church historically has been biblical in its perspective. Black people have also understood the Bible differently from whites. They have, without question, read and studied the same words of Scripture as whites; however, blacks have discerned a different message in the same words. That is why Nat Turner, a religious man, preacher, and visionary, led the insurrection in Southampton County, Virginia. He felt he was doing God's will— ushering in an age of justice and freedom. However, his white slave master felt that he was mentally unbalanced—a vicious psychopath. Black preachers have historically been the social philosophers of the race.[21] They have found in Scripture a ray of hope that has enabled them to confront the systemic ills of American society and interpret the biblical message in light of the social reality.

The contemporary conservative evangelicals, represented by well-known televangelists and others, use the same language as black preachers but generally mean something totally different. This is why they are so dangerous. Consequently, blacks need to understand that there is a difference in how words are used and the point of reference involved. Clearly there must be a wrestling with the question of how two people are able to say the same thing and mean something different.

We live in an age when weapons that destroy and kill are called "peace keepers," and governments that enslave and oppress claim to be fair and just. Likewise, when evangelicals say, Jesus can set you free, they tend to mean that his power enables one to be redeemed and therefore set free from an individual catalogue of personal sins such as lying or lusting. When blacks say, Jesus can set you free, they mean this in a holistic way, including personal sins but also actual freedom from social, economic, and political bondage. Evangelicals tend to dichotomize their understanding of the gospel, to act as though social realities and spirituality are two mutually exclusive phenomena. Blacks maintain the interrelationship between evangelism and the social realities of one's life. Likewise, the black preacher is concerned not only with the soul but with body and soul, spiritual food as well as rice and potatoes—food that will keep the hungry child from dying or stealing. We believe that religion and life are tied together and should not be separated.

This is the real, practical struggle—to balance the tension between what popular and traditional evangelism espouses, which is biblically narrow and semantically misleading, with what is ethically right, just, and fair. Blacks are not seeking happiness in the Aristotelian sense; however, they indeed are worthy of happiness in the Kantian sense if anyone else is. To be happy is to be Christian and free in this world, here and now.

Evangelicalism

From the inception of broadcasting the Word of God, this new phenomenon in religion, there have been skepticism and questions regarding its impact upon the local congregation. Denominational ministers worried about the effects of broadcast religion on traditional church attendance and participation. While the more mainline ministers hedged on participating in the electronic ministry, some evangelicals eagerly seized the opportunity to be heard. Paul Rader's program "The Breakfast Bridge" was the first religious program to be heard on the CBS radio network in the 1930s.

Although the concept of "church" had not been conceived as a part of religious broadcasting, it was looming in the backs of the minds of some evangelical preachers. However, radio as a medium of communication does not engage people in the same manner as television. Its programming is structurally passive while television is action oriented and demands a higher degree of participation. Television destroys obscurity and visual anonymity, requiring such smoothness in style, dress, and demeanor that acting and image become necessary in its participants. Television has transformed religion into a type of show business—a very big business allowing some religious media masters to gross millions of dollars annually.

Although the careers of many television and radio evangelists have spanned much of this century, for example, Garner Ted Armstrong, Billy Graham, Oral Roberts, and Fred Price, their influence has not been as widely felt as that of Pat Robertson, Jerry Falwell, and, until recently, Jim Bakker. The electronic visibility and the political and economic clout wielded by these individuals are unmatched in the history of television religion. These popular and contemporary television evangelists espouse a very conservative and oftentimes simplistic view of God and the world. They reach more people than ministers in local churches could ever dream of reaching. Moreover, they have a negative effect on the local church which is manifested in reduced contributions and a quest for simple approaches to ministry and social problems. We suspect that a significant number of persons contributing to these televangelists are black and poor—people who can hardly afford to support their own families and the local church, much less the televangelists. Nevertheless, they are doing it and this is the lifeblood of these programs.

Those who contribute knowingly or unknowingly perpetuate the conservative political philosophy and theology espoused by these evangelists. Money, therefore, acts as an extension of the "gut feeling" of the contributor and subsequently sanctions the actions or program of the person or organization to whom it is donated. Money that is not donated to any specific cause, but used to advance one's own product or ideology, has the same effect, but instead of being objectively influential, it is subjective. More precisely, money enhances the message of any medium and, as a medium itself, its message is intricately connected with a medium such as television. The reason companies pay very high prices for thirty-second commercials during the World Series, Super Bowls, and "Dallas" is because millions of viewers watch these programs and can be influenced by advertising. The high cost of these commercials is directly related to the number of viewers. Marshall McLuhan points out:

> "Money talks" because money is a metaphor, a transfer, and a bridge. Like words and language, money is a storehouse of communally achieved work, skill, and experience. Money, however, is also a specialist's technology like writing; and as writing intensifies the visual aspect of speech and order, and as the clock visually separates work from the other social functions. . . . It is action at a distance, both in space and in time. In a highly literate, fragmented society, "time is money," and money is the store of other people's time and effort.[22]

Money indeed enables one to propagate an ideology, and it has a unique relationship to numbers of people. In the case of televangelism, the number of people donating money shows that crowds and money strive toward increase. The amount of money involved is incredible and we suspect that some blacks who refuse to tithe or give to the local church are contributing to their favorite television preacher.

The televangelists' use of the most sophisticated technology to convey the "simple gospel truth" is self-contradictory and self-righteous. It is self-contradictory because the gospel does not offer simple answers to complex problems. However, it does encourage folk to strive toward unity and peace through what the Greeks called agape. *Agapē* or the love of God which informs all other forms of love enables evangelicals to understand that Jesus and the gospel encourage and demand action to help the poor and oppressed achieve equality and fairness. Self-righteousness is sin and it replaces the righteousness of God with the unquestioned exaltation of self.[23] Inasmuch as many modern evangelicals seem to feel that they possess a monopoly on morality, acting as though their views are the only ones right for the country, they are self-righteous and more sinful than the persons and policies they castigate and deplore.

In the national election of 1980, Jerry Falwell's Moral Majority supposedly was instrumental in the defeat of several liberal Democratic senators, namely, Birch Bayh, George McGovern, and Frank Church. Some of these men accused the Moral Majority of circulating literature that labeled them as "baby killers" and instilled in the minds of some voters the notion that they were immoral.[24]

The influence of Moral Majority on the outcome of the election met with mixed interpretations, yet Peter Galuszka quotes Jerry Falwell on November 6, 1980 as saying: "It was the greatest day for the cause of conservatism and American morality in my adult life. . . . Ninety percent of the candidates preferred by Moral Majority won."[25]

The conservative evangelical movement is a religious and political force that can only be accurately measured as the future unfolds. Its use of technology and other media, its financial holdings, political clout, and persuasive power over a significant number of people contribute to the present reality of the movement's success. The future may render its present "success" or "progress" a fad or an illusion but only the future can accurately characterize its impact upon the United States and the world. The recent fall from stardom by Jim and Tammy Bakker as well as the media explosion surrounding Oral Roberts and his "seclusion" to inspire more financial contributions as well as the political aspirations of Pat Robertson let the world know that the impact of the television evangelists, preachers, or commentators is growing in visibility and influence.

Empty Religion:
Form without Power

There are indications that suggest that a growing number of people desire to be mesmerized by the shallow fervor of some of our religious leaders— especially the televangelists. This desire and participation have reached astounding proportions when compared to traditional religious expressions. However, the Scripture warns: "You must understand this, that in the last days distressing times will come. For people will be lovers of themselves, lovers of money . . . haters of good, treacherous, reckless . . . holding to the outward form of godliness but denying its power" (2 Tim. 3:1f., 5). People are turning to easy ways of expressing their religious interest, concentrating on and being impressed with form and not content. Indeed, both are important and neither is fully adequate without the other. Yet we are too quick to accept form only. The word "form" is used to mean style without substance. Therefore, we often concentrate on the form of religion at the expense of the content. Paul, in writing to Timothy, is concerned about this to the extent that he accused those who held to the forms or outward semblance of religion of "fundamental insincerity."

Empty religion is religion with form and only form. It purports to be the gospel, yet it disregards the whole message of Jesus Christ, a message filled with the power of God and the power of the Holy Spirit, a message concerned with justice and the abolition of oppression. Empty religion is marginal religion; it is doing just enough to appear righteous, while the heart of our lives is stained with the blood of corruption and our tongues are drenched with the venom of deceit and double-talk, a poisonous and deadly posture. Empty religion is form without power! It is powerless because it can be loud or quiet; it can be somber or jubilant; it can be many things, but it is not powerful enough to transform the lives of people. It has no transformational power because it has form without substance. What we mean is simply that empty religion is religion that essentially accepts the condition of society as normative. Empty religion is spirituality without social consciousness. It is worship for personal satisfaction without believing that we are all tied together by the power of God who is no respecter of persons. In Jesus, there is no hierarchy of importance, no distinction between human beings. "There is no longer Jew or Greek, there is no longer slave or free, there is no longer male and female; for all of you are one in Christ Jesus" (Gal. 3:28).

The black church is not exempt from this criticism because there is a tendency among clergy and laity to be superficial and flamboyant. Few black ministers on radio and television are preaching liberation messages, urging the church to be an active agent of social change, opposing morally wrong and insensitive policies of government and industry. If every black preacher in America decided to confront seriously the status quo through sermons and programs that advocated protest against our cavalier treatment of the poor, we could begin the process of transforming the condition of life for the oppressed of society. This radical approach to ministry would enable the church to reclaim its heritage as an institution that has been on the cutting edge of social change. This radical approach may mean that preachers will have to sacrifice popularity, acceptability, and personal success for the good of the black community as a whole—embracing a limited, yet appropriate, understanding of John Stuart Mill's utilitarian doctrine of "the greatest good for the greatest number."

This means that some of the symbols of achievement and progress will have to be redefined in light of the goal of transformation. For example, the preacher's Cadillac as a symbol of prosperity and progress may have to be abandoned. The building fund, which in many churches is more sacred than the Holy Bible, needs to be reevaluated. Some churchgoers seem to be more willing to contribute to a building fund than they are to give toward the transformation of lives or to support the gospel ministry. Accordingly, the building fund has in effect become a way of subverting the gospel of transformation. The church has learned how to pretend to do the work of the ministry while embracing an egoistic and capitalistic approach to evangelism. In practice, this means the church and its leaders funnel money through the building fund in order to avoid a theology that will really help change the lives of people. Then we rationalize this behavior by arguing that certain programs cannot be funded because there are not enough capital resources to provide for the hungry and shelter the homeless or help others on the long and difficult road toward self-determination and self-sufficiency.

We must add, however, that the black church is proud of its independence and rightly so. This may account for the almost irrational and irreligious regard for the building fund. It has been a means for churchgoers to establish their autonomy and independence. The building fund, however, need not have precedence over missions and the goal of transforming the condition of life for blacks in America. The building needs to be the headquarters for the practice of liberation.

Religion that commercializes God's power through selling prayer cloths and other gimmicks is laden with emptiness. It is without power, yet gullible people are being influenced and persuaded by these prepackaged messages accompanied by glamour and technology. This is precisely what some black and white evangelicals do in their speeches and homilies. Their language is consoling and familiar but their meaning is misleading because their actions are not transforming the lives of the victims of oppression or the victimizers. These evangelicals do not understand that evangelism is trans-formational. Accepting Jesus Christ and the essence of the gospel message is radical because it means that our lives should indeed change and our response to society should be different. "So if anyone is in Christ, there is a new creation" (2 Cor. 5:17). This newness means that transformation has occurred. It means that people have become committed to social change through understanding that Jesus is the model for a more perfect order— one that confronts the status quo and endeavors to transform the world to a place where justice, fairness, equality, and moral rightness become a reality.

Why do blacks bother to participate in something that is too simple and too easy to change their social situation? To some extent the black church is like children dancing to any tune and responding to the lyrics of a death song. The religious practices of the evangelicals do not possess or expect to possess any transforming power in favor of the oppressed. A religion that is not empty is one where individuals and institutions experience the words of Paul when he says, "Everything old has passed away; see, everything has become new" (2 Cor. 5:17). This includes the social structure as well as our individual selves. Our love of others becomes new; the indifference and selfishness are to be done away with. If these things that constitute one's attitudes have not changed, if one's baptism has not renewed one's life, then that one is not truly in Christ and not a new creature, but the same old person.

Paul said to the Corinthians, "If I speak in the tongues of mortals and of angels, but do not have love, I am a noisy gong or a clanging cymbal" (1 Cor. 13:1). In other words, Paul is saying that emptiness pervades the church. Likewise, the Old Testament prophet Amos could say to those who were so interested in form and not the will of God, "I hate, I despise your festivals, and I take no delight in your solemn assemblies. Even though you offer me your burnt offerings and grain offerings, I will not accept them. . . . Take away from me the noise of your songs; I will not listen to the melody of your harps. But let justice roll down like waters, and righteousness like an everflowing stream" (Amos 5:21-24).

Religion must be concerned with justice and righteousness. If it is to be authentic, it needs to take issue with form and appearance, and in order to be prophetic, it needs to be able to see emptiness for what it is and dare call it that. Conversely, religion that is not empty is religion that has power. It is powerful enough to make us change our social and political situation in America. It gives us the power to seek freedom. Religion that has power is the voice of truth cutting like a two-edged sword, yet healing the wounded by the power of love and compassion that only comes through Jesus. It is religion that knows that the blood of Jesus allows us to be saved from the grips of injustice and oppression as well as sin. Powerful evangelism understands the message of Jesus as one that transforms the church and world by upsetting the status quo and requiring that freedom and justice become a present this-world reality.

Social Change and Black Liberation

Many things are changing at a pace that is quite fast and difficult to monitor. Only twelve decades ago, blacks were enslaved in the United States, most people lived in rural areas, transportation was by horse and buggy, and public education for everyone was basically nonexistent. We can reflect upon certain phenomena that have changed drastically during our own lifetime. Today most families have telephones, television, videocassette recorders, automobiles, wives working, children in day care, and a host of other modernities that were not around only a decade or two ago.

Heraclitus, several centuries before Jesus Christ, indicated that change is constant.[26] The nature of change has intrigued thinkers and philosophers almost from the beginning. However, during the time of Heraclitus, another thinker, Parmenides, argued that reality only appears to change—change is actually impossible.[27] Later, the reflections of the philosopher contained in the Book of Ecclesiastes offer a similar perspective. "A generation goes, and a generation comes, but the earth remains forever. The sun rises and the sun goes down, and hurries to the place where it rises. . . . What has been is what will be, and what has been done is what will be done; there is nothing new under the sun."[28] The wisdom expressed by Parmenides and the writer of Ecclesiastes is both profound and disturbing, true and false, assuring and doubtful. Both permanence and change are synthesized in nature, however, in the atomic theory.

Social change is a more difficult phenomenon because change that deals with people's attitudes, prejudices, and practices is more complex. How does social change occur and to what extent? Certainly new laws are written, the constitution is reinterpreted, new findings are made, and new decisions are rendered. The law, however, does not change the way people really feel. The law is more a reflection of change than an agent of change. Change comes from within the heart and soul of like-minded individuals.

Radical social change—that is, change in society that will affect the reality of discrimination and poverty by limiting their impact on black people—certainly has not been achieved through the evangelicals nor the black church. Only recently have black theologians advocated such change. J. Deotis Roberts in *A Black Political Theology* has said that "the black church needs a theology of social change and political action."[29] Moreover, in my view, the church has to become an active and intentional agent of liberation and social change. It must be the catalyst that will foster social change as a continuous phenomenon until the reality of equality is evident in all areas of life for blacks and minorities.

Traditionally, the church has played an important and much needed role in the lives of blacks. However, the signals of the church have not been so clear that the perpetrators of oppression and injustice would know unequivocally that the black church will not be a passive participant in oppressing its own people by acquiescing to the alluring power of the status quo. Certainly there have been preachers who have led the effort to bring about liberation and change—Nat Turner, Richard Allen, Peter Spencer, Marcus Garvey, Martin Luther King, Jr., and a host of others. But the spirit of protest and the essence of dissent have not been institutionalized in the black church in order to sustain the image that persons such as Turner, Allen, and King presented. The radicalism practiced by these black leaders has not been sustained, and without sustained protest and rebellion there can be little or no lasting change in the social condition of the impoverished and oppressed.

Why did the Reagan administration's justice department fight so vigorously to create "neighborhood schools" while saying nothing about discrimination in housing? Why have the rights of the individual been usurped and relegated to a lower status? Certainly, black people in America become outraged. How long will blacks passively accept their social condition in America and the condition of their black brothers and sisters throughout the world? What will it take to evoke a response that will not be apathetic and torrid, but bold and courageous? Constructive and controlled anger is needed to provide the impetus for social change. Blacks need to demonstrate anger, disgust, and disapproval of their social condition and stop acting like they are happy and content.

It is generally understood and accepted that people in power do not relinquish that power without a struggle. This struggle can take the form of physical, emotional, psychological, economic, racial, religious, or legal confrontation. Inasmuch as blacks are alienated[30] from the mainstream, the only way that we are going to change the situation of oppression and injustice is by pushing and shoving and making our presence felt and heard on issues of religious, social, and political significance. I believe that the liberation of blacks in America, South Africa, and other Third World countries is directly related to the black church. The black church needs to lead the way in this protest because it has the requisite degree of independence to make a difference once the commitment is made.

The Black Church and Christian Freedom

Christian freedom is somehow perceived as unrelated to freedom in a sociopolitical context. Whites have been able to institutionalize racism by dichotomizing everything, namely, church versus state, religion versus politics, and freedom "in Christ" versus freedom in the particularity of one's social existence. However, let me affirm forthrightly that Christian freedom is not a mysterious state of spiritual bliss grounded in a personal experience of Christ that can be isolated and privatized as many evangelicals would have us believe. Any personal experience with Christ is also an experience with truth that releases us from bondage. This is not simply a bondage of personal sin but bondage in general—spiritual, social, political, and economic. Jesus' first recorded public message was a message of freedom. "The Spirit of the Lord is upon me, . . . He has sent me to proclaim release to the captives and recovery of sight to the blind, to let the oppressed go free" (Luke 4:18). In John's Gospel, Jesus says, "The truth will make you free," (8:32b) and, "So if the Son makes you free, you will be free indeed" (v. 36). These passages speak quite clearly to the concept of Christian freedom.

Over twenty years ago, preacher and prophet of justice and social change Martin Luther King, Jr. wrote that "Freedom is one thing—you have it all, or you are not free. Our goal is freedom."[31] As one of the most inspirational thinkers of modern times, King was certainly correct in his assertion that we must set our eyes on freedom and strive to achieve it as a goal. The attainment of this necessary goal requires struggle and commitment. Nevertheless, I often wonder if blacks today have the same goal that Dr. Martin Luther King, Jr. expressed. Is freedom, with all of its concomitants and attendant circumstances such as justice and equality, something that we are working actively to achieve? The goal of freedom cannot be accomplished by osmosis or silent meditation. Black people know this all too well because three hundred years of history suggest that without a plan of action there can and will be no freedom. It is clear that freedom vis-à-vis attaining socioeconomic justice is a valid theological goal that blacks must actively seek without fear of retribution.

Black religion influenced by evangelicalism generally tends to be conservative and socially accommodationist. In this connection it has often-times quelled the rebellious spirit of blacks. However, some notable radicals such as Richard Allen, Nat Turner, Denmark Vessey, Gabriel Prosser, Henry McNeil Turner, Martin Luther King, Jr., and a few others have confronted the system because of its status-quo orientation and because of the tendency to regress toward docility and humility—a normative posture for the pious Christian believer. There is no historical precedence for blacks to expect social change to occur outside of the black church.

I believe that the black church has to take the lead in changing the social structure because whites have not and will not do it. The eradication of poverty, underemployment, joblessness, crime, low self-esteem, inadequate housing, and a host of other problems that plague the black community need to be actively addressed by the church because after three hundred years of unfreedom—from slavery to the new federalism—blacks continue to be oppressed in spite of the efforts that come from "Caesar's household." There have been some blacks who have succeeded in becoming mainstreamed and acculturated while others have sunk deeper into the quagmire of poverty and oppression.

Christian freedom is human freedom, and for the Christian, in the language of Ernst Käsemann, "Jesus means Freedom."[32] Traditionally, Christian freedom, like Christian theology and Christian ethics, has been affected by what Pierre Teilhard de Chardin has arrogantly called the "axis through the West." This is a way of indicating that authoritative and acceptable concepts and practices of religion, like other disciplines, have to be validated by a stamp of approval from the Western world—a world that pays little or no attention to or respect for the views of minorities. America, the leader of the Western world, set an example of this high-handed subjugation during the days of slavery and created a language veiled in simplicity yet confounded by obliqueness. "Christian Freedom," like the well-known phrase in the Declaration of Independence of the United States, "All men are created equal," is a victim of the intent to narrowly define and interpret freedom and equality not just under law but also under God.

This Orwellian doublespeak has indeed been around a long time. So when I say that blacks and whites mean different things when they use terms like "Christian freedom" and "equality," this should come as no surprise to anyone who has ventured to read the Bible or the Constitution. For example, scriptural phrases such as "slaves, obey your master" were used to justify the enslavement of blacks on biblical grounds. It was a part of God's divine will and plan that blacks should be subservient and docile, while whites would develop and apply the hermeneutical principles of interpretation. This "bourgeois privatism,"[33] still evident today, obscures the meaning of Jesus Christ as the paradigm of freedom and enables white and black conservative evangelicals to unjustifiably dichotomize Christian freedom and human freedom.

Jesus' message in Luke 4:18 is one that gives hope to those in bondage and enables the discouraged, dispossessed, and disenfranchised to believe that he is the model for understanding freedom. Moreover, the words in the Gospel of John, "the truth will make you free," clearly equate Jesus with truth and suggest that he is the means by which freedom can be accomplished: "I am the way, and the truth, and the life" (John 14:6). Christian freedom is directly tied to Jesus as the model for excellence. He is the one who reversed the prevailing perceptions and practices by setting a new standard (cf. Matt. 5:21-22, 31-34) and by speaking with authority. Jesus' message and his actions represented freedom. He felt free to be a friend of tax collectors and sinners and to readily associate with those who were castaways. His followers, that is, Christian disciples, can in the words of Martin Hengel find "freedom from domination."[34] Clearly this freedom is the essence of Christianity—human relationships are based on the ability to pursue one's rightful goals and purposes without the fear of subjugation and oppression. Christian freedom is a freedom that extends beyond human sanctions and is conferred upon those even in bondage. This means that the modern slaves are not just blacks, but also white oppressors who are themselves held captive by the "will to dominate." This will to dominate others is the essential manifestation of sinfulness because it contradicts the expressed purpose of Jesus' earthly ministry, which was to set people free (Luke 4:18).

Actually, Christian freedom is not a black or white issue—it is a human issue. It is a relationship with Christ that necessarily enables us to respect all of God's children regardless of race or social status. Yet "freedom is seen as freedom from sin and freedom from obedience."[35] Clearly the will to dominate others is sinful, and Christians have to be liberated from this sinful and egoistic practice. Through Jesus Christ, we have been set free from sin and death (cf. Rom. 8:2-4). But how do we reconcile this dialectic of freedom with the fact of oppression and injustice that still prevails and is often perpetrated by those who likewise claim to be Christians? This is the dilemma that faces the black church in America.

Christian freedom is evidently understood differently by blacks and whites. This is partly due to the cultural and experiential differences between the groups. Whites who are socially, politically, and economically free are comfortable in thinking of Christian freedom as freedom from personal sin because they have rationalized sin to be more a catalogue of "dos and don'ts" than a state of separation from God (Gen. 3:8-10). Moreover, blacks, who have historically been in bondage and continue to be disproportionately poor and victims of the free enterprise system, tend to understand Christian freedom as human freedom. James Cone makes a similar point in referring to how black slaves and white slave masters had a different view of God because their experiences were different. He writes:

> The life of a black slave and white slaveholder were radically different. . . .
> The life of the slave was the slave ship, the auction block, and the plantation regime. It involved the attempt to define himself without the ordinary historical possibilities of self-affirmation. Therefore, when the master and slave spoke of God, they couldn't possibly be referring to the same reality.[36]

I am concerned about the black church and how it can bring about change in itself, the local community, and the larger society. Karl Marx described religion as an opiate of the people, and to a large extent blacks have proven him to be right. Blacks who are systematically oppressed have romanticized their suffering for too long. Now is the time to develop a new approach to the social ills that are disproportionately inflicted upon blacks in America. This rebellion needs to start in the church and make its way into the structure of American society. I believe that black liberation theology offers the theoretical foundation for the black church to develop a model of social change that will liberate black people from the social malaise that holds the black church and the black community hostage.

The church has the potential to make a difference in a sociopolitical system that subjects black Americans to oppression. Liberation of black people throughout the world can only come about when blacks decide that "enough oppression is enough," and I believe that the church has the power spiritually, economically, and numerically to accomplish this freedom. An old song of the black church tradition says, "This joy I have, the world didn't give it to me. The world didn't give it and the world can't take it away."[37] In the same spirit of protest and assurance, I say that our freedom has not and will never be given to us by the wielders of power. We need to take it upon ourselves to chart systematically the course of freedom with the assurance that Jesus Christ is indeed on our side.

The Gospel and the Oppressed

The message of Jesus is one that is addressed to the despised and oppressed. He comforts and strengthens the weak, feeds the hungry, and heals the sick of their diseases—those who are on the "underside of culture." Jesus concentrates on tax collectors, sinners, and those who have been treated as second-class citizens (cf. Luke 7:22; Matt. 21:31). Black liberation theologians such as James Cone, Gayraud Wilmore, and J. Deotis Roberts, along with other liberation theologians like Leonardo Boff, Gustavo Gutierrez, and Jon Sobrino have consistently pointed out that the message of the gospel uniquely addresses the situation of blacks in America and poor people of Latin America and other Third World countries.

More recently, Jens Glebe-Möller in his book *A Political Dogmatic* joined the voices of conscience and change by stating that God's kingdom means liberation (freedom) for those who are now oppressed and plagued by the inequities that exist in society. He quotes Edward Schillebeeckx: "Hurtful master-servant relationships must not exist in the Christian congregation. The New Testament thereby indicated that in practice the kingdom of God consists in not only inner renewal but also renewal and reform of the social structures."[38] Basically, this is exactly what the message of Jesus *was* and still *is* about. His words tend to "turn things upside down." His sayings such as "So the last will be first, and the first will be last" (Matt. 20:16), and "You have heard it said of old, but I say unto you" in addition to parables of reversal (cf. Matt. 20:1-13; Luke 14:1-24; 15:11-32; 16:1-21) indicate a cataclysmic change in the social structure. Moreover, the theme of the gospel or Jesus' own systematic theology constantly addressed the needs of the poor, the oppressed, the sick, and the weak. Therefore, James Cone is again correct in saying:

> Jesus had little toleration for the middle- or upper-class religious snob whose attitude attempted to usurp the sovereignty of God and destroy the dignity of the poor. . . . The kingdom which the poor may enter is not merely an eschatological longing for escape to a transcendent reality, nor is it an inward serenity which eases unbearable suffering. Rather, it is God encountering man in the very depths of his being-in-the world and releasing him from all human evils, like racism, which hold him captive.[39]

Jens Glebe-Möller essentially corroborates what Professor Cone maintains when he writes:

> When Jesus forgives sin, it is once again those who are ideologically and socially the lowest in the pecking order, or of no rank and status whatever, that he addresses himself to. What does this say? It says that he gives them, on behalf of God or of the kingdom of God, their only possible chance for a future. To the others, those who are religiously or socially or economically "well off," he has nothing to say.[40]

The gospel is basically a message of freedom from oppression and injustice. Jesus is overwhelmingly concerned with those on the bottom of the socioeconomic ladder—those "tax collectors and sinners" Jürgen Moltmann has described.[41] This same message is buried within the pages of Adolf Harnack's classic, *What Is Christianity?* The gospel is a message of liberation and social change that focuses on freedom from the structures of injustice. It clearly favors those on the "bottom side" of the economy. "The gospel is a social message, solemn and overpowering in its force; it is the proclamation of solidarity and brotherliness, in favor of the poor."[42] Moreover, the message of the gospel has not changed, and the social context of blacks in America is still one of oppression and injustice in spite of the fact that a number of blacks no longer feel a kinship to poverty and deprivation. These "Negroes" have essentially been brainwashed by their new gentrified status, and now believe that material success and opulent living are proof of God's favor toward them. They believe that if they could get a college degree and a good job, then everyone should be able to do the same. However, they fail to acknowledge the systematic nature of injustice and oppression. They are the black conservative evangelicals who are more interested in personal gain and individual salvation than in the collective freedom of black people.

In cities throughout America, the homeless and the poor seek food and shelter. People are sleeping in the cold and eating the refuse discarded by those who live poshly and in glitter. Today, in a land "flowing with milk and honey" the numbers of poor are increasing steadily. This contradicts the often-held belief that a job is the answer to the problem of getting people off welfare.[43]

There is a real need to allow the message of the gospel to speak to our current situation. This gospel message allows us to see and understand that Jesus Christ is indeed the liberator. Latin American theologian Jon Sobrino, in referring to Jesus, says:

> It is the *poor* that He addressed his mission in a special, privileged manner, it is with them that he lives; it is for them that he posits the signs of the coming of the Kingdom miracles, the expulsion of demons, wondrous food and drink. It is from a starting point among the poor that he denounces the basic sin and tears away the mask from rationalizations of that sin. Because of all this he comes into conflict with the mighty and is persecuted to death.[44]

To understand the gospel is to understand Jesus as a friend and advocate of the poor and oppressed. Christian freedom, then, has to be understood in this context because before there can be a true and just understanding and praxis of liberation, our christological understanding of Jesus has to reflect an appreciation of his revolutionary words, "He has sent me . . . to let the oppressed go free" (Luke 4:18).

This is the gospel—the good news that true evangelism must espouse. This is the message that Jesus practices in his life and preaching. If there is a kerygmatic, evangelical message that is true to the historical, observable praxis of Jesus, then it must be a message of liberation. Any message about Jesus that refuses to acknowledge the radical and transformational content of his ministry and message must be seen as something less than the gospel of Jesus Christ.

A true evangelist has faith in the gospel and proclaims that gospel. The word "gospel" comes from the Greek noun *evangelion* which means "glad tidings, good or joyful news, or gospel."[45] Therefore, a truly evangelical message is a gospel message. A gospel message is a message about Jesus Christ, the lamb of God. Ultimately, a message about Jesus is a message of liberation. Blacks should never talk about Jesus without talking about freedom and liberation from poverty, injustice, and structural oppression.

Conclusion

Clearly, there is a continuing need for evangelism and the evangelization of blacks. Evangelism is a significant part of the church's ministry and mission. There is a need to hear whatever message is being heralded to change the plight of black people who are disproportionately represented on the bottom side of the economy and the social pecking order. Without question, the black church has provided a message of hope and inspiration. However, J. Deotis Roberts is correct when he states that "Evangelism among blacks must be more than telling the old, old story. Without our deeds of caring and giving, our telling is mere verbiage; full of sound and fury signifying nothing."[46]

All our lives, we have heard sermons about salvation from sin and the need for faith. Revival messages and Sunday sermons will forever ring in our ears and soothe our souls. Yet the reality of black life is that it is poverty-stricken and below the level of whites with similar or matching characteristics, for example, education, family size, and gender. For well over three hundred years now, the black preacher has preached, the choirs have sung freedom songs, and the sisters and brothers in the congregation have shouted and rejoiced while the nature and structure of oppression simply adapt to the prevailing social norms. There is a need for something more basic to happen than simply to worship in the traditional fashion and to return for the same thing on the next Sunday.

Gayraud Wilmore is astutely correct in his assessment of how black churches and their leaders assimilate the practices of white evangelicalism rather than try to develop the church's awareness of oppression and injustice. In criticizing some of the more vocal opponents of black liberation theology, Cone quotes Gayraud Wilmore, saying:

> It is not because black theology is obscure, unbiblical, or has no doctrine of the church but because the majority of black preachers confuse themselves with Billy Graham and the most unenlightened versions of white evangelicalism. Because they do not know the rock from which they were hewn, they and their people do not know who they are and the inheritance that was passed on to them by men like Benjamin Tucker Tanner, William W. Colley, and Alexander W. Waters. Because they have an understanding of redemption that cannot admit the sanctification of secular conflict and struggle.[47]

This is indeed the harsh reality that describes some of what goes on in black practical religion. Individual church revivals, citywide revivals, and crusades have made the black church similar to its white counterpart. Pastors know that much of what the black church does locally and nationally is accommodationist, that is, the minister tends to do what he or she perceives to be the expectation of the laity, rather than develop in the laity a new understanding regarding liberation practices. Not only that, there also seems to be a tendency to accommodate the prevailing social structure rather than taking the risk to force change.

Let me affirm that this assessment or self-criticism does not take anything away from the contributions that the church has made or is making to meet the many needs of its people. However, I believe that evangelism in the black church has to take seriously the true meaning of the term, which points to the gospel or "good news" of Jesus Christ which is liberation- and freedom-oriented. This means that the church cannot simply be interested in increasing the numbers of persons who attend its worship services and prayer meetings. Numerical growth is only one measure of effective evangelism. But when persons do come to church, they will have to be taught the meaning of community, fellowship, freedom, liberation, and cooperation. The good news does not enslave, but frees people to love and work together for justice and righteousness. It does not conform to prevailing perceptions and actions, but transforms people and the structure of society. Evangelism is not the act of passing out tracts about what others have said or simply inviting people into the church with a revolving door. Evangelism is witnessing to the transforming power of God as Peter and John did when they stated, "For we cannot keep from speaking about what we have seen and heard" (Acts 4:20). They had seen and heard that the name of Jesus transforms and frees people.

2

The Urban Community

How very good and pleasant it is when kindred live together in unity.
—Psalm 133:1

We do not live to ourselves, and we do not die to ourselves.
—Romans 14:7

Confess your sins to one another.
—James 5:16

To exist in community is to live in relationship to Christ. Living in relationship to Christ, however, is to be in relationship to the children of God regardless of their socioeconomic status, skin color, education, or family background. Practicing the Christian faith which is an expression of our love and understanding of Jesus Christ is the binding force that makes community possible. Commitment to the principles of Jesus and a willingness to practice his teachings will hasten the day that genuine community will be a reality.[1] Dietrich Bonhoeffer said, "Christianity means community through Jesus Christ. No Christian community is more or less than this. . . . We belong to one another only through and in Jesus Christ.[2] Unfortunately, Western culture has perpetuated a sense of separation and superiority that puts one person above another—white over black, man over woman. For example, today many older white people have had little to do with people of color, except as servants. Blacks entered their homes through the back door in order to raise their children, scrub their floors, cook and clean, and do whatever they demanded. As a child growing up in Virginia, I remember my father refusing to work for whites. He would get angry whenever anyone asked my mother to do domestic work. He thought it was better to be poor and self-determined than to be personally dehumanized by whites and Jim Crowism. These whites sit in church every Sunday seemingly oblivious to the fact that professed faith must be practiced in order to be meaningful. Samuel Proctor makes this point clearer by stating that "Christianity has been diluted over and over, as a moral force, by those who were fervent in their profession but flaccid in their practice."[3] When these same oppressors get old and feeble, the only persons that their families can get to take care of them are blacks. What an irony!

The truth of Scripture is borne out in human experience. We do indeed live and die in community, not alone. But what kind of community do we exist in? Is it really community when we are only related or held together by self-interest, egoism, and individualism? Even within the local church, there is an abundance of disunity often fostered by the creation of more groups. For example, some churches have five to ten choirs, some of which have been formed out of controversy, discord, and the inability to work together. It is distressing to observe in the church—the community of faith— a blatant example of the lack of community as evidenced by the fragmented, individualistic, autonomous nature of groups and auxiliaries. Each group functions as if it were unrelated to the whole. This unfortunate reality in many churches fosters competition and resentment. Some pastors and parishioners perpetuate this disunity by encouraging a competitive spirit, and the phrase "We beat them" becomes the rallying cry of church-sponsored contests.

The black church today needs to focus its energies on unity and togetherness and not succumb to the lure of sensationalism and competitiveness that characterize the market economy. We do not live to ourselves because we belong to the Lord, and if we live, we live to the Lord (Rom. 4:7-8). To live to the Lord is to recognize that the Lord is the source and strength of our lives, and the life of others is as important to God as our own lives.

The Meaning of Community

Those who live to themselves not only live without friends and family but also without God. The words "We do not live to ourselves" imply that not only do we need other people such as family, friends, and even strangers, but we certainly need God. We cannot ultimately live without the hand of God in our lives. Therefore, "We do not live to ourselves" is an exhortation against selfishness—against the pride that Reinhold Niebuhr discusses in *The Nature and Destiny of Man*.[4] To live to oneself is to be too proud of oneself, thereby living out of fellowship with others.

This type of pride is human presumption and self-glorification. In the book of Isaiah it is described as the ground of sin. The prophet says, "The haughty eyes of people shall be brought low, and the pride of everyone shall be humbled; and the Lord alone will be exalted in that day. For the Lord of hosts has a day against all that is proud and lofty, against all that is lifted up and high" (Isa. 2:11-12). The prophet Amos echoes the same sentiment, saying, "The Lord God has sworn by himself says the Lord, the God of hosts: I abhor the pride of Jacob and hate his strongholds; and I will deliver up the city and all that is in it" (Amos 6:8).

This sentiment is echoed throughout the Old and New Testaments. In 1 John we again find similar words: "For all that is in the world—the desire of the flesh, the desire of the eyes, the pride in riches—comes not from the Father but from the world" (1 John 2:16). To live to oneself is to exclude God and everyone else. Living thus becomes a manifestation of what we can justifiably call false pride. To live to oneself is to deny the words of the psalmist, "How very good and pleasant it is when kindred live together in unity!" (Ps. 133:1).

Yet, many say, I am going to live my life the way I want to—I'm going to look out for number one. This is the "me, myself, and I" posture that Robert Ringer discusses in his book, *Looking Out for Number One*.[5] When blacks embrace this attitude, they fail to come to grips with the fact that Jesus was not self-centered but focused on self-denial for the good of all humanity. Jesus did not live to himself, but lived in community with tax collectors, sinners, lame persons, the blind, poor, and the hungry. In essence, he lived in community with all of God's children. In humility, he always pointed to God, saying, "The Father is greater than I" (John 14:28), or "Not my will, but yours be done" (Luke 22:42). In the same spirit, we need to understand that the power of God enables us to be who we are. This means that when our lives are going well, and when we have given to the poor, fed the hungry, and visited the sick, these things have been accomplished by the power of Jesus Christ who enables us to live in community with others. God's grace enables us to cast off our egoism and become humble. When we do good to others, we are only doing what we would have them do for us.

In addition, Paul says, "We do not die to ourselves." Like life, death also involves others—the Christian community, the family, and friends. Whether we live for God will determine whether we die for God. If we live for self, then we shall also die for self. We need to realize that death only cancels out life in terms of the body; it does not cancel out the content of our faith and character or the memory of our actions.

There is a need for the church and urban community to understand their interdependence. Neither the church nor the community lives to itself. A new sense of interdependence will enable blacks from all segments of society to understand anew the words of Paul to the church at Rome: "We do not live to ourselves, and we do not die to ourselves. If we live, we live to the Lord, and if we die, we die to the Lord; so then, whether we live or whether we die, we are the Lord's" (Rom. 14:7-8).

Faith and Self-Help

The church has historically balanced its Christ-centered worship and theology with a quest for social and political reform in the community. Blacks rightly believe that Jesus is concerned with fair treatment, right action, and instilling moral responsibility in people by teaching and preaching a message of redemption and transformation. Regretfully, we know that personal spirituality is often oblivious to the need for doing what is morally and ethically right in the community. This is why we can assert that there are far too many people who have had a religious or spiritual transformation that is confined to the self in that they have not related this new belief or perspective to the external world. Therefore their internal change has not really altered their worldview. They continue to "see through a glass darkly" (1 Cor. 13:12, KJV), and in the process fail to link evangelism with the eradication of poverty and oppression. This "born-again" status does not change their approach to oppression and injustice. Somehow they do not relate their introverted religious experience to the external world.

Christian religion is not limited to what the white church perceives as legitimate religious practices. The black church has its own perspective about religion which includes liberation and change as a legitimate goal of religious practices and faith. To some extent, the church has been instrumental in bringing about freedom and equality since the days of slavery. The history of the black church's concern with social change is well documented. From Richard Allen to Nat Turner to Martin Luther King, Jr., black religious leaders have fought for their people to be released from social and political bondage. The religion of the slaves was not just a spiritual phenomenon that omitted the reality of their condition. It was also an agent of change. Though the white slave masters wanted religion to be an opiate[6] that would seduce blacks into accepting their status and keep them docile, some blacks found in religion and the Bible the motivation to be free.

However, slave religion was effectively used as a method of social control to promote the status quo. Vestiges of this mentality still exist in the black church because in spite of the contributions of the church in fostering change, it remains a silent and cooperative institution. As a matter of fact, some of us in the black church believe that it is more in complicity with the status quo than an opponent of it. This may or may not be intentional; however, the church is not actively protesting social ills such as segregated neighborhoods, neighborhood schools, at-large city elections, lack of proportional hiring in government and industry, racial discrimination in higher education, income discrepancies between blacks and whites, warehousing blacks in public housing and public schools, and a host of other conditions that disproportionately affect the black community. Even during the height of the Civil Rights struggle, when racism and oppression were blatantly represented by Jim Crow laws and overt hatred, the black church was reluctant to launch an all-out war against the status quo. What Gayraud Wilmore has called the "deradicalization of the church"[7] has caused it to be socially and politically conservative. The church is no longer a serious threat to the establishment because it has become establishment oriented, failing to provide the radical voice needed to bring about meaningful liberation and change in American society.

Nevertheless, the black church is a powerful force in the lives of black people, but the question is, How much of a change agent is it? Is it really capable of changing the social and economic face of urban America? I believe that this is possible because the church has a rich history and its present numerical and spiritual strength is unmatched in the black community.

> Few institutions have played as great a role in the lives of black Americans as the church. Along with meeting the spiritual needs of its members, it is a major social, political and economic force in black communities. Much of the church's strength lies in its members, and in terms of membership, it continues to thrive: there are an estimated 18 to 20 million black Christians in the U.S.[8]

If the spiritual, social, intellectual, economic, and political energies of our people could be harnessed in such a way that a black local, state, and national agenda could be developed in order to change our life situation, then the United States would never be the same. There would be a change in the distribution of wealth, burdens and benefits, perceptions of power and strength, and so on. This change would occur according to the best American tradition—from the grassroots of American society to those who occupy the pinnacles of power.

T. J. Jemison, president of the National Baptist Convention, U.S.A., says, "The black church is the strongest organization among black people, but it has not asserted itself in the manner that I feel it should. It has not used the power of its numbers to lift the standard of living for black people."[9] This sentiment was echoed by the late Bishop Frank N. Reid, Jr., former head of the Council of Bishops of the African Methodist Episcopal church. He said, quite correctly, "We must fervently and passionately return to the principles of earlier black leaders. Chief among these principles are the ideas of self-help and community involvement."[10]

The idea of self-help does not suggest that external forces, that is, governmental programs, and so forth, are not necessary nor does it imply that blacks should be expected to do everything for themselves while other groups are assisted by federal programs. This is not meant to be a naive assertion that fails to understand the endemic nature of the problems that pervade the urban centers of the United States. However, blacks must remember that neither government nor anyone else has been committed enough to growth and development to effect the cataclysmic changes that will foster substantive progress in the employment status, education achievement, income level, and reduction in crime rate in the black urban community.

Though some conservatives may espouse a self-help philosophy, their reasons are far different from ours. We are convinced that the black community must cross the psychological threshold of believing that we can make a real difference, by ourselves, in our socioeconomic condition and plight. An internal initiative or a positive implosion of energy and excitement based on faith and self respect will enable blacks to eradicate the torpor and malevolent attitudes that grip so many in our community. The myth of substantive external assistance needs to be recognized for what it is. For over three hundred years, blacks have received little help toward achieving freedom and equality. History alone substantiates the need for blacks to reevaluate the power inherent in the church and community if the condition of black life is to be transformed.

The church has a rich and difficult past; however, the present and the future need not reflect poorly on past experience. The new prophetic vision is one that will enable the black church to be a more powerful force than even its history can claim. Consequently, the church should not be a haven of refuge from the destructive and oppressive forces of American society. Instead, it should be an active force calling for major changes in the economy, work force, political parties, and governmental agencies vis-à-vis a major internal change in the focus of ministry.

The Introverted Church

As an institution, the church consists of individuals with separate attitudes, instincts, and functions. However, as a whole, the church displays a predominant psychological attitude in the same sense as individuals. Using Carl G. Jung's two basic types, termed introverted and extraverted, the church can properly be characterized as introverted because it is subjective in its focus and actions with little commitment to change or compulsion to address external stimuli. Applying Jung's archetypes, the black church can be described as the "introverted feeling type." In describing this type, Jung rather chauvinistically indicates that he found a predominance of introverted feeling types among women. Few black preachers can argue with the fact that women constitute an overwhelming majority in the church and are its actual power base. Jung describes this type in the following way:

> They are mostly silent, inaccessible, hard to understand; often they hide behind a childish or banal mask, and their temperament is inclined to melancholy. They neither shine nor reveal themselves. . . . Their outward demeanor is harmonious, inconspicuous, giving an impression of pleasing repose, or of sympathetic response, with no desire to affect others, to impress, influence or change them in any way. . . . Although there is a constant readiness for peaceful and harmonious co-existence, strangers are shown no touch of amiability, no gleam of responsive warmth, but are met with apparent indifference or a repelling coldness.[11]

I think some of these characteristics can be used in describing the church as a collective entity. The church acts like an independent entity, divorced from the suffering of the external world. It is basically silent, peaceful, and harmonious—failing miserably to understand the need to abandon its neutrality on issues of social and political justice. The introverted church is subjective and egoistic, basking in the beauty of its bricks and mortar and the melodious syncretizing of its chancel choirs, pipe organs, and grand pianos.

This introverted behavior may contribute to numerical growth and internal excitement. It does not foster the liberation of the oppressed because the focus is too concentrated on the church as an individual institution, secure in its own rituals and practices. Hendrikus Berkhof in his book *The Doctrine of the Holy Spirit* has related this introversion to the church's neglect of the spirit's mission in the world. He states, "In neglecting rather than reflecting the great movement of the spirit, it distorts the whole content of faith and is an accomplice to the individualistic and institutionalistic introversion and egotism still found in the churches of today."[12]

The black church is compelled to become an extraverted institution—one that will take more risks, demand more justice, and force blacks and whites to move beyond personal conversion to community transformation. To do this, it will have to change its focus of ministry. Rather than emulate the privatistic, personal model represented by modern evangelicalism, it needs to hear anew the great commission in Luke 18:29 and Jesus' message of liberation in Luke 4:18. Moreover, the message of the prophets—though often dogmatic, hortatory, and searingly blunt—needs to be revisited by both preacher and laity so the themes of justice, righteousness, doom, judgment, and liberation can help the church tear down its walls of isolation and individualism.

The concept of community needs to be expanded to include the whole community—the church and the world. However, as long as the church is introverted and parochial in its approach to ministry, it will continue in its failure to effect liberation and change in the United States and the world.

Between Church and Community

The black church recognizes that it cannot afford to remain an isolated institution. It needs to begin to perceive itself as an integral part of the political, social, and economic system. Unless the church recognizes this, it will remain a virtually powerless institution in terms of its ability to bring about liberation. However, if the church sees itself as outside or above this system, it is doubtful that it will ever become the kind of force that will help change our society. In order to understand the roots of the problem and fashion a solution, the church needs to understand the political and economic forces that act upon it and what it can do to make a difference in the social structure.

The black church in the United States is appropriately described by pastors, laity, and other observers as the most independent, self-determining institution in the black community. The active laity in these churches is numerically overwhelming and there are millions of others who are basically unchurched. However, the black church is only a potential power broker reveling in quasi-individualistic forms of worship and programs that have historically failed to substantially address, much less alter, the basic social condition of most of its constituents. For example, pastors and laypersons are compelled to ask, What is the value of anniversary banquets and testimonials? How important are fellowship services and pulpit exchanges in enhancing community and fostering liberation and change? Can social change occur across denominations in cities and towns throughout the United States while the black church is busy bartering and selling dinners as a way to meet budgetary needs? How long will churches ignore the issues of discrimination, unemployment, teenage pregnancy, poor and inadequate housing, substance abuse, and crime that grip the black community? Too many pastors and denominational leaders have parochialized the ministry and failed to see the connection between ministry and social change, theology and transformation, and the church and the urban environment. There is a serious need for black pastors to conceptualize the black community, the mission of the church, and their pastoral roles in much broader terms. The present autonomous engagement is too limited and prescribed to significantly affect the social climate of urban America.

What is needed is a new type of linkage and interdependence between the church and the black community. This will help advance the quality of life of all blacks and hasten the process of achieving equality, fairness, and peace in our communities. More important, there is a need for a new prescriptive theology—one that will help to usher in a new day of freedom, justice, and equality. The genesis of the black church is found in the cooperation of the oppressed. The economic survivability of the church and the community is grounded in a mutual understanding of the need to help each other advance beyond their present status. Historically, mutual aid societies or beneficial organizations grew out of the church, as did most early social organizations. In this connection, F. Franklin Frazier, an outside critic of the church, pointed out quite some time ago that

> it was in order to establish their own churches that negroes began to pool their meager economic resources and buy buildings and land on which they stood. As an indication of the small beginnings of these churches, we may note that the value of the property of the African Methodist Episcopal Church in 1787 was only $2,500. During the next century the value of the property of this organization increased to nine million dollars.[13]

The ability of blacks to work together and survive is rooted in history. Slaves developed ingenious means and methods of survival. Their descendants, current black church leaders, are compelled to develop creative and innovative ways to improve the social, economic, and political status of blacks in American society. Joseph Washington corroborates the assertions of Frazier. "The independent black churches brought to life black folk religion and the black cult. Black mutual aid societies, charities, relief and all forms of organized social life for the improvement of the community were rooted in the churches, the birth place of all sources of value."[14]

Inasmuch as the church is the value center of the black community, it needs to evaluate the present situation, that is, the status of the community, and determine what viable course is necessary in order to begin the process of transforming the socioeconomic and political status of blacks. There is a critical need for the church to play a major role in shaping and determining the destiny of blacks. This will demand reorientation and a new understanding of progress. The modern church community has to recapture the spirit of protest and discontent that characterized the early church in the black community. The illusion of power and success has to be overcome, and we need to face up to the prevailing reality of oppression and injustice in order to fight against this cunning yet vicious monster called malaise and apathy.

> The authenticity of black folk religion is the unity between spiritual and social powers which finds expression in the first blush of the independents—the coming together for ameliorating suffering. It went further. The black church in the period of slavery attacked it as an institution with both its clerical and lay members involved in abolitionist movements and the underground. Black churchmen were the unsung heroes of the thirty years preceding the civil war. Black churches were the backbone of educational and political development of black Americans.[15]

There remains a great deal of pain and suffering in the black community, and urban America continues to be a bastion of poverty and unemployment, while the church languorously acquiesces to these conditions as if they were an inevitable concomitant of existence. The number of persons hungry and without shelter is growing, and churches are bombarded with a barrage of poor seeking to be fed or assisted in numerous other ways. This suffering cannot be dismissed with nonchalant disinterest by those of good will and moral conscience. The church is called to creatively and compassionately seek solutions to these problems and not to succumb to the luring power of indifference enhanced by an individualistic quest for comfort and power. To some extent, we have long been on the cutting edge of fostering change. However, the struggle for freedom is no less necessary today than it was in the past. If history is to be our teacher, we must understand that the struggle for freedom is a continuous process that requires the active and radical participation of the church.

The segregation of America's cities, the resegregation of some public schools within systems declared unitary, crime in the streets, and poor and inadequate housing are realities that must be confronted with new and creative solutions. The masked inequities and subtleties of discrimination that allow only a few blacks to penetrate the upper echelons of the public sector and the corporate suites create the grand illusion of equity and fairness. The "acceptable," "safe" individuals who have been put in positions of authority and power must not use their new status to humiliate and oppress other blacks. Instead, they have a moral responsibility to make innovative strides toward helping the masses who still languish in poor housing, illiteracy, unemployment/underemployment, and the lack of adequate health care.

Ambivalence and Dilemma

The black church is an amalgamated entity—a plethora of individuals with relatively common interests and experiences. However, black Americans are the products of a dual system of justice and fairness in all areas of their experience. So the term "black American" is a semantically anti-thetical description of a person who is black first and American second. Blackness supersedes Americanness because history and present reality substantiate the refugee status of black people in America.[16]

Accordingly, I fail to understand black athletes or other stars who try to extrapolate their talents or accomplishments from their blackness as if there were no logical connection between them and their color. Likewise, there is a structural ambivalence in the hearts and minds of black church-goers mainly because of their contextual situation—a situation that is the result of a double standard, one for whites and another for themselves. This merely substantiates what W. E. B. DuBois aptly called "double consciousness."[17] Geneva Smitherman illustrates what DuBois meant.

> Thus, from the very beginning, we have the "push-pull" syndrome in black America, that is pushing toward white American culture while simultaneously pulling away from it. . . . A striking example of the phenomenon is the ex-slave Absolom Jones, founder of one of the first separate black church movements within White Protestant denominations. Jones took on the white man's religion, and proceeded to practice it. (The "push"). Yet when he attempted to pray in a white church in Philadelphia in 1787, an usher pulled him from his knees and ousted him from the church. Thereupon, Jones along with another ex-slave, Richard Allen, established the African Methodist Episcopal Church. (The "pull").[18]

The push-pull or double consciousness is what I call ambivalence. It is a state of existence characterized by the inability to be absolutely sure of the desire to be black and deal with the consequences. Moreover, it is fence-sitting—keeping one foot in the black community while the other is trying to escape to the world of acceptability among whites in terms of socioeconomic and political compatibility. No matter how determined one's efforts to become acculturated or assimilated into the mainstream of American society, the color of one's skin will remain black, which means that in the United States black people will have minority status until such time that we become a majority.

In my book *Black Ministers and Laity in the Urban Church* I also argued that ambivalence exists among clergy and laity in the urban church.[19] The results of the survey simply offered statistical verification for what DuBois and more recent scholars have correctly asserted. The dilemma or ambiv-alence is a uniquely black phenomenon—a moral problem with concrete consequences. This is indeed something that blacks did not learn from whites because white America has never had a problem with the double standard that was practiced toward blacks. The Declaration of Independ-ence—a document laden with language of high moral quality and sound theological judgment—did not affect how whites perceived blacks and neither did it prevent the practice of a double standard. The language of manhood and equality vis-à-vis God-given rights was never intended to include blacks. Peter Paris makes this point with superb clarity.

> Contrary to the general opinion among blacks, white America experienced no dilemma between its theological thought and the way it treated blacks. For white America it was not a matter of believing in true justice while practicing injustice. Rather, in that respect, the white churches experienced no alienation between their thought and practice. This is evidenced by the fact that any attempt to preach racial equality in the pulpits of white churches has always been viewed as an act of hostility against their prevailing ethics. Since blacks assumed a static theology that transcended both races, they inevitably concluded that racist activities were deliberate violations of professed theological beliefs. They had forgotten that Christian churches ostensibly had no difficulty with slavery for centuries prior to the abolitionism of the nineteenth century. In fact, it is highly doubtful that the New Testament itself offers unequivocal opposition to slavery. Thus if slavery had such a long history among Christians, one should not suppose that Christians would necessarily believe themselves to be under religious obligation to treat ex-slaves as first-class citizens.[20]

While blacks labored over a double-consciousness, whites practiced a double standard. The moral and theological dilemma for blacks provided no such complications for whites. The black church continues to be soaked in a sea of uncertainty. It is partially stifled by ambivalent feelings regarding its involvement in social and political practices while simultaneously doing the evangelistic work of the church, testifying and making a conscious effort to save the world from sin. "Unfortunately, the black churches also failed to perceive that ecclesiastical theology necessarily arises out of the activities of the churches and not vice versa."[21]

Black Religion in the City

Black urban churches must become more interested in liberation and social change because the black community currently neither reflects a thorough understanding of its problems nor has any prescription for solving them. Our urban populations have until recently reflected the general belief that peace as a national goal is unimportant and unattainable and social problems are the norm. The cities of our nation are faced with economic, social, and political problems that equal and to some extent surpass the problems of an earlier era. There has been a national trend toward state's rights as evidenced by the New Federalism and a growing neoconservatism. Moreover, there is an effort to turn back the clock in public education, affordable housing, and race relations. The practice of blatant racism as evidenced in 1987 by the residents of Forsyth County, Georgia, or Howard Beach, New York is symptomatic of a nation that continues to harbor vestiges of the resentment and hatred that characterized three hundred years of history for blacks in the United States. National leaders, including the president, have not spoken emphatically against these practices. Moreover, there is a gun-toting mentality among the young and old; the United States Justice Department has led the way in establishing neighborhood-schools policies. This is a major policy shift because in the early 1980s the United States was espousing a domestic policy that supported integration in housing and education. The shift to a neighborhood-schools policy is government-endorsed segregation. Consequently, neighborhoods throughout urban America remain visibly segregated, and unemployment among blacks continues to be disproportionately high. These are some of the problems that hold blacks hostage in a land flowing with milk and honey.

What is the black church doing to alter the conditions that affect so many of its constituents? Is the church a comfortable institution basking in its own glory, or is it again caught off guard? More important, is it too much a part of the system that needs to be drastically changed? Over twenty-five years ago, in 1963, Dr. Martin Luther King, Jr. described the church in words that are searing and indicting. In his "Letter from Birmingham City Jail," a masterfully written philosophical treatise, he writes, "The contemporary church is often *a weak ineffectual voice with an uncertain sound. It is so often the arch-supporter of the status-quo. Far from being disturbed by the presence of the church, the power structure of the average community is consoled* by the church's silent and often vocal sanction of things as they are."[22] Dr. King's words echoed the disappointment of many young blacks with the church during the early sixties. However, in the eighties, the church can still be described as part of the status quo. But this will have to change if blacks are going to play a major role in transforming their present situation from a despairing, unemployed, subsidized consumer to a self-determined contributor to the community and church.

The Bible makes several references to the city and its inhabitants, corruption (Isa. 1:21-22), oppression (Amos 2:6f), and injustice. Moreover,

the Biblical mandate for urban ministry can be seen in two topics. First is the Scripture's appeal to the city itself—with all its institutions—by the Old Testament prophets and the New Testament apostles. Second, and far more weighty and complex, is God's concern for justice for the poor and oppressed. His concern that the powerless members of society be treated fairly and with compassion is seen in numerous passages in both testaments and in the practices of the Israelite culture and the early church. Finally, and most powerfully, God's concern has been demonstrated fully in Jesus Christ.[23]

Inasmuch as black church theology is Christ-centered, Jesus is also the model for community transformation. The church is compelled to face the reality of the urban condition—a reality that is shaped by alarming statistics regarding unemployment, high school dropouts, and the growing problems of teenage pregnancy, substance abuse, and other maladies that plague the black community. The church has an ethical responsibility to protest against this awesome reality and endeavor to embark upon a systematic effort to turn the community around.

The Urban Reality

One of the world's greatest church fathers, St. Augustine, Bishop of Hippo, argued that without justice, the polarity between person and person would be exacerbated. In his classic book, *The City of God*, he declares that "justice is the first condition required for the existence of the city." However, the black urban community has been victimized by the lack of justice manifested in neglect, which has resulted in the city becoming the paradigm of polarity. Urban decline is directly and indirectly related to the injustice and inequality that have burdened blacks since they arrived in America as indentured servants who later became slaves. Urban decline is the result of many factors, including neglect, injustice, and attitudes that harbor vestiges of the past.

Moreover, "the term urban decline embodies the idea that declining cities are cities in trouble, cities not economically or socially healthy as they used to be or as they should be."[24] The predominant measure by which urban decline is frequently assessed is the loss of population. This form of outmigration is perceived as decline because it implies that the city is an undesirable place to live; it is also symptomatic of more pervasive urban difficulties. In this connection urban decline describes the city aesthetically and numerically vis-à-vis references to changes that affect how it functions. "Thus urban decline has both descriptive and functional meanings. In its descriptive sense, it refers to any decrease in such measures of size as population or employment. In its functional sense, urban decline means changes that somehow impair the functioning of a city or other urban agglomeration."[25] The most obvious and available measure of descriptive urban decline is a decrease in the total population. Yet a loss of population does not necessarily mean or imply a loss in the number of households. In some cases, there is an asymmetrical relationship between population and households. "The average number of persons per household fell 5.7 percent from 1960 to 1970, and another 12.4 percent from 1970 to 1980. Consequently, in many cities the total population is falling but the number of households is rising."[26] Population loss affects the production of goods and services by reducing employment opportunities. Also, outmigration from central cities is higher among whites than minority groups. "Among whites, the net migration rate from central cities to suburbs was 8.16 percent from 1970 to 1973, and 8.0 percent from 1975 to 1978. Among blacks, it was 0.3 percent from 1970 to 1973 and 2.9 percent from 1975 to 1978.[27]

Katherine Bradbury, Anthony Downs, and Kenneth Small point out in their book *Urban Decline and the Future of American Cities* that there are positive and negative effects of the concentration of poor and minority group households in urban areas. "On the plus side, minority groups have been able to exert more political influence in such cities and to advance to higher positions in government . . . than they would under a local government more dominated by whites."[28] However, there are some negative effects because

> the isolation of blacks and other minority groups tends to be increased, thereby reducing their mobility within the larger society. Concentration of large numbers of poor households in a few deteriorating central-city neighborhoods tends to produce a "critical mass" of adverse conditions. Also, the higher proportion of children from less affluent households in the public schools creates difficult educational problems. Many of these children come from homes not strongly oriented toward education. Recent evidence suggests that such children can be taught effectively but their concentration in certain schools often causes teachers and administrators to have low expectations concerning their performance.[29]

Furthermore, where persons live within the city is evidence of social stratification. There are real differences in treatment of persons from the poorer areas of town because they either look poor or speak without refined diction. A more precise indicator of differences is perceived when one gives his or her address. This information erects or overcomes barriers depending upon the perceived reputation of the community. "The residential differentiation extant in the society concerned is reflected in a sifting and sorting of populations and locations. As the city develops, types of population and certain systematic relationships between geographical space and social space appear."[30] Furthermore, where one lives is such an indication of social status that differences in people, at least socially, are readily presumed. Residential segregation tends to make these differences more discernible. Duncan Timms states that

> an address is far more than a convenient way of organizing the supply of public services or of locating an individual in physical space. It also locates him in social space. The address of a person immediately identifies him as a member of a particular social group. . . . So pervasive is this effect that

residential location has frequently been used as one of the measures in an individual's position in the local prestige hierarchy.[31]

In addition, some believe that "in order to preserve social distance, it may be necessary to institute physical distance."[32]

These arguments have been used in discussion and consideration of housing projects. The racial composition of these housing communities is extremely homogeneous. Herbert Hill states that

> concentration of low-income families in projects has the effect of isolating them from the general community. The huge size of the projects, structurally ugly and prison-like in appearance, set them and their residents apart from the surrounding neighborhood and the larger community. Erected in over-crowded slum areas, the projects stabilize, expand and intensify the existing pattern of de facto segregation. Huge structures built in areas of Negro population concentration insure an almost total preponderance of Negro occupants regardless of a city's avowed racial policy toward integration.[33]

Unlike other public assistance programs—namely, food stamps, Aid to Dependent Children (Welfare), Medicare, Medicaid, and so on—in which whites are recipients in greater numbers, public housing is mainly occupied by blacks. This suggests that in housing, the one area where family solidarity and stability are aided most effectively, blacks are most dependent. This also indicates that "homelessness" is an explosive and devastating problem for black America because those who are at the mercy of government programs are extremely vulnerable and susceptible to displacement.

The issue of affordable housing for poor and black people is a serious one that the church will have to face and help solve. The question is: How should the black church respond to this growing urban concern? There is indeed a need for a creative and innovative approach. The numbers of blacks with talents and abilities are legion. The time has come to pool the intellectual, spiritual, and economic power of the black community in a self-help effort to alleviate the problems that we face. The black bourgeoisie and the black masses, working in harmony with the black church, are capable of changing the face of urban America if they work collectively and are not ruled by the rugged individualism and the Protestant work ethic that have historically failed the black community.

The Neoconservatives and the Urban Milieu

The neoconservatives, in the language of Peter Steinfels,[34] believe that "equality of opportunity" should be granted to minorities. At the same time, they feel that there is too much welfare mentality in the United States.

Neoconservatives are indeed the academic elites who were once characterized as "liberals." However, the neoconservatives do not believe in "equality of condition" or "equality of results." In effect, they believe in justice without equality. Steinfels's explanation of the neoconservatives indicates that they are (Democrats, Republicans, etc.) committed to criticizing and analyzing any program that concentrates on the structural ills of this society, that is, racism, injustice, poverty, and so on, and offering solutions that tend to blame the victims rather than the oppressors. Moreover, they believe that the Great Society failed; instead of helping, it made people more dependent upon government. Accordingly, they assert that oppression and injustice are to some degree imaginary and the social ills that plague our society are well on their way to being solved. However, we feel that the neoconservatives are dangerously unconcerned about the poor, oppressed, and minorities. Moreover, they certainly are not really new; their latent ideas are just becoming more fashionable, and they are setting a national trend in the way that America views the disenfranchised inhabitants of the cities.

Nathan Glazer, in his article "Limits of Social Policy"[35] attempts to explain away the pathological problems of poverty, racism, and so on that are endemic to this society by pointing out the obvious. The human species has an insatiable desire or need to use very limited resources. Glazer indicates that we have limited resources, knowledge, and capabilities, and that "over-extension" is a part of the problem in the United States. Indeed, he indicates that the Vietnam War and the Great Society could not simultaneously reap positive results. To that extent, he is correct that the Johnson administration's war on poverty and other programs that characterized the Great Society were more political than substantive, more placating than eradicatory. They were designed to allay the unrest and social upheaval brought on by a failed domestic and foreign policy.

The crux of Glazer's argument is that the social ills structurally embedded in this society cannot, indeed, will not be resolved via social programs and policies because the machinations and mechanism designed to rid those ills are not capable of doing so. Glazer, like most of his cohorts, believes that the efficacy of social policy is not adequate to handle persistent social problems.

We are creatures of limitation—finite in all areas—and our transitory nature and whatever else that limits us is not sufficient reason to be dogmatic about the inability to cure the social ills of our time. The social ills that plague and haunt our cities need to be addressed by the church. The Neoconservatives are persistent in their claim that government "overload" is apparent and that the government cannot solve the social problems that permeate every fiber of our society. We vehemently disagree with the reasons and motives of these policymakers; however, the time has come for blacks to look within our own heads and hearts for solutions to the problems that beset us. The church and the entire black community have a responsibility to conquer the debilitating forces that impinge upon their freedom. We must be self-determined to transform our present status from dependence to independence, from oppressed to free.

The Black Church and Social Policy

One of the key public policy issues of our time has dealt with the question of fairness regarding equal opportunity in employment and affirmative action. Because the level of unemployment among blacks is disproportionately high, this is a critical issue for the black church and the black community. "Just as medical treatment is based on a diagnosis, affirmative action is based on the nature and extent of race, sex, and national origin discrimination. Affirmative action has no meaning outside the context of discrimination, the problem it was created to remedy"[36] Affirmative action, like busing school students for the purpose of desegregation, is a volatile and divisive issue which needs to be discussed and understood by the black urban church. Those who oppose affirmative action are quite vehement in their belief that it is another form of discrimination. We shall discuss the prevailing public view and then indicate the role that the black church should play in this social policy issue.

There are at least two types of objections to affirmative action that can be described as philosophical and practical. In both instances the intent is to truncate any efforts to establish an egalitarian society where blacks will be socially and economically equal to whites.

First, there is a large and growing number of conservatives and neo-conservatives who assert that preferential treatment or quotas are inherently unfair because they give preference to one group or race over another. They argue that this method of achieving equal opportunity is odious and invidious because it seems to establish a criterion for dismantling the vestiges of discrimination that is no less objectionable than the barrier that is being dismantled. In other words, these critics argue that discrimination cannot be fought with discrimination, and they feel that establishing quotas is the essence of invidious discrimination. Nathan Glazer, Daniel Patrick Moynihan, and Morris Abrams articulate the neoconservative position and its vehement objections to preferential treatment of blacks and minorities.

Second, there are others who passionately assert that discrimination is nonexistent in our present society. Yes, discrimination used to exist, but now things are positively different. Others, like George Gilder, view discrimination as a myth. Gilder's book *Wealth and Poverty*,[37] which was often called the Bible of the Reagan administration, argues that discrimination has been abolished in the United States. Moreover, he indicates that racial and sexual discrimination are also myths in the United States. Those who are black and must live with the subtleties, innuendo, and blatant acts of discrimination feel that the formulators of these arguments are insensitive and immune to understanding the way that blacks continue to suffer.

Affirmative action should be the essence of equal employment opportunity. However, aside from what it should be, it is an effort to eliminate the vestiges and causes of endemic discrimination in every phase of society. From the outset, equal opportunity in employment was in effect passive acceptance of past inequities while agreeing not to perpetuate or aggravate the said inequities. Therefore, equal employment opportunity is in effect an acceptance of the status quo. Conversely, affirmative action is an active, systematic program instituted to redress grievances and to hire and promote a proportionate number of minorities. The problem with those who oppose affirmative action is related to the fact that Americans still believe that justice and fairness, concepts ingrained in the constitution, are somehow exclusionary. The white American public and its leaders refuse to understand that affirmative action is a moral responsibility that seeks to give meaning to the concept of fairness and the practice of justice. The opponents of affirmative action argue that meritocratic standards are in existence in the public and private sector. These persons optimistically believe that there has been a tremendous decline in discrimination in America, thereby refusing to acknowledge the level of subjectivity inherent in any merit system. Philosophically, affirmative action is an effort to comply with the mandate of justice which implies fairness to all. Affirmative action programs tend to temper the subliminal belief held by some blacks that failure is contrived, whether it relates to tests, selection, promotion, or any other factor. These programs tend to instill hope and some degree of trust and faith in a system that blacks view with skepticism. This mistrust of bureaucracy and power as well as a legal system that has historically fashioned its laws to truncate the aspirations and hopes of blacks and minorities has caused many to live in despair and hopelessness.

Moreover, affirmative action is an egalitarian process of effectuating change in the long-standing employment, educational, training, and general personnel practices in government and the private sector. It is an attempt to comply with the effort to create a society that is not hindered by the lingering effects of slavery, institutional racism, and the Dred Scott Decision of 1857. Any realistic analysis of the intricate machinery developed and perfected over a two-hundred-year period to deny the essence and existence of blacks should suggest that "business as usual" will not suffice as an effort to correct such practices.

With this understanding, we surely take issue with Nathan Glazer, who in *Affirmative Discrimination* seems to argue that individual opportunities are encouraged and acceptable while group goals or statistical parity are somehow unjust and therefore discriminate in reverse.[38] Glazer seems to deplore proportionate hiring or selection because it appears to circumvent the meaning of "qualifications" and "equality." He and others need to be reminded that blacks as a group are the most economically, educationally, and physically deprived people in America, with the possible exceptions of Native Americans. Moreover, the legacy of slavery and the effects of legalized disenfranchisement cannot be overcome by the illusive nature of equal opportunity. Blacks have been subjected to the most dehumanizing experience of any American inhabitants—legal, educational, and moral debasement documented by over two hundred years of slavery.[39]

The black church has a responsibility to teach its constituents the value of economic interdependence so blacks can launch an all-out effort to become producers and not simply consumers. The process of education is important here because schools and other institutions are not cncerned about teaching economic independence or interdependence. It is up to the black church to systematically redirect the energy and thought process of its members beginning when they are very young. When children say that they want to become firefighters and police officers when they grow up, they need to be challenged then to become producers of goods and services so that they can help change the status quo. Other professions and careers need to be romanticized and glamorized by blacks so the community will not continue to be laden with dependency and poverty. The number of black firefighters and police officers is still disproportionate to the population; however, becoming a firefighter or police officer is not economically lucrative enough to help the black community out of its political and economic impotency. The church must be the new inveigher against the malaise that has invaded the black community, and against the continued oppression that runs rampant in our cities.

The Church's Role in the Urban Situation

How does the black church alter the policies of the state? What effect can the church have on policies that tend to treat blacks as insignificant? The question that Martin Luther King, Jr. asked twenty-five years ago is as appropriate now as it was then. "Is organized religion too inextricably bound to the status-quo to save our nation and the world?"[40]

Black and white churches in the United States are too detached from the world to realize that their silence regarding the myriad problems of our society is in effect collaboration with the perpetrators of injustice. In any sizeable American city there are thousands of people who are actively involved with the church; however, most are not seriously concerned about the poor. The church needs to challenge individuals to evaluate and determine their commitment to social, political, and economic issues. For example, during the February 1987 Black Theology Project at the Interdenominational Theological Center in Atlanta, the Reverend Mac Charles Jones and others poignantly pointed out the need for economic development within the black church and community. Moreover, Joseph Washington has edited a monograph, *Black Religion and Public Policy*, that offers several suggestions about how the black church can influence and change policy.[41]

The church needs to radicalize its perspective regarding its role as an institution and begin to understand its strength in order to change the nature of urban America. It needs to become a social force—one to be reckoned with by the wielders of power. This will mean that worship and other religious activities will be only a portion of the church's agenda. There will be a new focus and commitment to change via education and organization.

Even worship now does not acknowledge the presence of oppression and injustice. The sermons of black ministers take on a new social and political focus when racism and injustice are confronted from pulpits. The focus on Jesus and the kerygma must not be isolated from the reality of poverty and oppression. The presence of demeaning and repulsive urban conditions needs to be addressed in the message of salvation and redemption. The black minister cannot morally or politically afford to be oblivious to the reality of the urban condition and preach as if the goal of black people is to be mesmerized into an otherworldly frenzy without a real concern for eradicating the dehumanizing force of the present.

How important is it to boast of a church with three thousand members if they are not being challenged toward freedom and self-determination? What is the value of large collections if the money is not fostering economic independence and development? The prophet Amos, in chiding the Israelites, spoke harshly to those who were comfortable with injustice while glorying in their worship. The heart of his preaching is found in the following words:

> I hate, I despise your festivals, and I take no delight in your solemn assemblies. Even though you offer me your burnt offerings and grain offerings, I will not accept them, and the offerings of well-being of your fatted animals I will not look upon. Take away from me the noise of your songs; I will

not listen to the melody of your harps. But let justice roll down like waters, and righteousness like an everflowing stream.

(Amos 5:21-24)

Clearly, the mandate of the prophet Amos still holds today because there remains a need for justice and righteousness to prevail. The church has a responsibility to its constituents and to the larger society to help transform our society into one where liberation and justice will be realized during our lifetime.

Bureaucracy and Indifference

The time has come for us to recognize that the bureaucracies we help create and depend on are initially more involved with controlling rather than facilitating change. This is why I believe that the black church must come to understand that the hope of real liberation and change resides in its own people. Those of us who labor in the trenches of ministry, where practical theology is born and nurtured, must begin to put forth a church theology of liberation and social change that will free blacks from the violent hand of indifference and apathy. The black church has the responsibility of teaching its constituents that government is not helping them to become free. The few welfare dollars and other subsidies are not raising the standard of living for the masses. The church must teach its people how to study day and night, pray unceasingly, work two or more jobs doing whatever it takes to survive and succeed, in order that we will not be forever confined to the fringes of society, that we will not depend upon the hand of indifference and injustice to be benevolent toward us.

The mentality that believes that somehow we are and will be helped by an external force has no historical precedent for black people. We have historically worked long and hard for the wealth of others. And while the United States government gives billions of dollars to sustain the economies of other countries, it is doubtful that it will ever give the resources needed to create strong, healthy black communities. Certainly God has helped and will help us. Moreover, our faith enables us to believe that God will be with us "from everlasting to everlasting," but God also helps those who help themselves.

There is something assuring, albeit deceptively false, in believing that we live in a society that provides for the basic needs of citizens who are "less fortunate" and equally supplies jobs for those who want to work. It is comforting to think that those who are "truly needy" can qualify for our benevolence. But we need to remember that we live in a system where government programs reflect our desire to moderate the negative consequences of social change. And it is not just the government that does this—so do other established institutions, even the church.

Today, recipients of welfare and food stamps typically are employed, but earn wages so low that they continue to qualify for benefits. They are indeed the "working poor," as Sar Levitan and Isaac Shapiro have told us.[42] Blacks have always known from their experience that working does not mean that one will no longer be poor. Small subsidies are provided through public benefits which have the expressed purpose of "aiding dependent children," but the ultimate consequence is governmental and bureaucratic indifference to the fact that minimum wages are inadequate to support a family or pay an average rent. Rents are sometimes subsidized through other public programs designed to compensate landlords for use of their property, which many tenants could not afford if forced to exist on current wages and employment opportunities. Food stamps, while having the side effect of providing a minimal standard of nutrition for recipients, mostly provide a subsidy for food producers and distributors. One subsidy is no more benevolent than another. Black and poor people clearly are not the beneficiaries of American benevolence. We need to dispel this myth!

In examining the nature of our social structure and how progressive changes are affected, it is important to look at the function of bureaucracy as well as the role our perceptions of it play in encouraging or discouraging personal involvement. Basically, we can assert that the United States is founded on a series of constitutional objectives: forming a more perfect union, establishing justice, ensuring domestic tranquility, providing for the common defense, promoting the general welfare, and securing the blessing of liberty for ourselves and our children.

To accomplish these goals society has established elaborate networks of organizations and programs administered by agents of the government referred to as public servants who direct the military, the courts, collect and distribute revenue, educate our children, maintain public property, protect us from crime, and regulate activities of citizens and other agencies. A small percentage of the government labor force consists of elected officials, those chosen to guide or create policy based on the perceived needs of a majority of the voters, and the more clearly expressed wishes of those who actively lobby to influence policy. This generally excludes blacks who neither constitute a majority nor have the resources to lobby as big business does. I submit that the business community benefits more from government benevolence than the struggling poor.

This social and governmental structure is large and extremely complex. Therefore, we need to examine results actually achieved through its processes. Providing for domestic tranquility and justice for all citizens are endeavors frequently in conflict. They reflect our desire for law, that is, due process, and other protections designed for the potentially innocent, and our societal need for order or a general freedom from undesirable social activity. The pursuit of both objectives is often emotional since each involves strong personal belief on the part of many individuals. For example, crime victims and their families often present very different perspectives on law and order from the views of civil libertarians or those wrongly charged with an offense. Providing for the common defense, though originally intended to supply resources should we be attacked, has meant many things. In some administrations this has meant pursuit of a noninterventionist policy designed to reduce the inclination to international hostility. In others it has been portrayed as the need to intervene on behalf of the national interests, which are more often economic than social, while developing an arsenal which deters hostile nations from acting aggressively. This is all quite arbitrary!

Finally, what is a more perfect union? Is this a joining of states where each relinquishes some autonomy in order to provide for the interest of all? Or is it the basic right of individual decision making, which acknowledges diverse common interests beyond state boundaries? All of these questions reflect some of the more pressing social and political dissension in our time, yet all revolve around reaching very basic constitutional objectives. Each objective, and each method favored in achieving it, is reflected in the organizations, policies, and individuals we have designated to obtain these basic ends. The black church needs to become a key actor in the process of objectifying these constitutional promises. It can no longer depend on the good will of others to do anything except look out for their own interests.

If we understand indifference as violence and bureaucracy as indifference, as some philosophers, theologians, and poets have, it is important that we examine the impact of our policies, and the institutions that implement them, in the context of two major and very abstract constitutional goals: providing for the general welfare and securing the blessing of liberty for ourselves and our children. This is important since during two hundred years of constructing policy from many perspectives and electing and appointing administrators with varying points of view, neither of these goals has been promoted for a significant portion of our society—namely, the black community.

Historically, the approach to dealing with the needs of the poor in the United States parallels that of seventeenth- and eighteenth-century England. During that period it was generally accepted as fact or divine providence that individuals were born into a specific economic status which was theirs till death. Aristocrats begat aristocrats, peasants begat peasants. Government assistance to the poorest citizens was a meager subsidy that merely prevented massive starvation and death in the villages.[43] Social policy was created to validate and ensure the status quo and was administered by those who benefited most.

Massive unemployment during the Depression, the inhuman conditions endured by both adults and children in the workforce, and a general disregard for equality gave rise to an increasingly hostile labor force during the 1930s and 1940s. Labor union growth, fueled by intense economic disorder, represented a potential threat to the economic and social status quo. To alleviate the consequences of poverty, which were more visible than its cause, social programs were created to provide minimum assistance. Like English Poor Laws, aid to the deserving was based upon age, illness or disability, and, for women, marital status. With minimum aid provided for the "most deserving" and jobs provided those willing to work under programs such as the National Recovery Act, American citizens were encouraged to believe, just as British citizens had some fifty to seventy-five years earlier, that employment or aid was available for any deserving individual. This is the myth.

The largest subsidy offered America's poor is payment for medical care through Medicaid and Medicare. Through these programs, eligible individuals, who actually constitute only a small percentage of those living below the poverty level, receive services for which doctors and other helping professionals receive hefty remuneration. All of these payments constitute "social spending," or payments we count as assistance to our country's less fortunate. They are in fact subsidies to the most fortunate who collect rents, medical bills, and other resources that would otherwise be unavailable. At the same time, individuals can avoid personal actions of benevolence, since the perceived existence of charitable programs relieves us of any moral responsibility. We are also led to believe that failure must be attributed to the recipients of our charity.

Whatever charity or benevolence that blacks receive will not transform their lives. The church needs to help blacks realize that outside help is not intended to foster freedom. It creates the illusion of progress, but in fact it is a part of the system that is to a large extent responsible for the state of existence in which blacks are saddled. The black church needs to begin to discuss and debate this issue with openness and clarity. Then we need to develop ways to help change the system so that it will deal seriously with the reality of urban poverty and bureaucratic indifference.

3

Black Theology

There needs to be a close relationship between theology and ministry. After some twenty years of the development of black theology, black denominations, pastors, and congregations are not greatly moved by the insights of black theology or black theologians. A way needs to be found to change this. There is no way fully to estimate the value of black theological reflection to the life of black Christians, to the ministry and witness of black churches. Theology has been not only a faith response but a thoughtful engagement with the souls of black people. It not only aids in assessing the signs of the time, it is deeply anchored in the roots of black culture, history and church tradition. It has much to offer to black people toward self-understanding and social transformation.

—J. Deotis Roberts,
Black Theology in Dialogue

Samuel Proctor, pastor emeritus of Abyssinian Baptist Church, says, and I agree, that black theology is a needed corrective to all bad theology, and that "all good theology should be liberating."[1] But the "correctness" and "goodness" of black theology need to be understood and practiced by the Christian community, especially the black church. Few ministers and laypersons who labor in black churches are aware that black theology is a discipline of study and reflection. Consequently, interest in and understanding of black liberation theology barely exists among the majority of persons that I have encountered in the black church. While my own contextual experience as pastor has been limited to a few thousand people, my colleagues in the practice of pastoral ministry corroborate this perception.

Furthermore, many black pastors still think that black academicians who construct theology outside of the practices of the church are largely out of touch with the very people about whom they claim to write. Because of this perception, few black ministers read and teach the works of prominent black theologians such as James Cone, Gayraud Wilmore, J. Deotis Roberts, C. Eric Lincoln, or Major Jones. Even fewer laypersons are familiar with the tenets of black liberation theology. I believe that the social and political life of black people can be transformed by bridging the gap between black theology and the ministry of the black church.

Theology and the Black Church

Theology is both an academic discipline and a practical responsibility of the church. In its pure seminary form, it is generally foreign to the church. After completing theology school, young ministers have to struggle to make their newfound knowledge relevant to churchgoers. Ordinary church-goers are not interested in the arguments or theories about the existence of God or the color of God. This does not mean that these questions, debated by philosophers and theologians, are unimportant. However, persons in the church, struggling to practice the Christian faith, *are* interested in what God has done and can do to help them with their particular concerns and problems. These problems are often related to sickness, hunger, death, family, housing, crime, and education. Black churchgoers expect the preacher to have the knowledge and faith to assure them of God's power, not to question or doubt it. What these laypersons need to understand is that the process of faith development may sometimes be enhanced by searching the depths of the soul for a more comprehensive understanding of the nature and power of God. The pastor can challenge the church to deal with the issues of injustice and oppression by using black theology as a method of teaching and preaching liberation.

Not only is it true that clergy and laity are, to a significant degree, out of touch with black theology, but some black theologians are also out of touch with the black church. Somehow, academic theology is thought to be more meaningful and profound than the practical theology that actually grows out of the black church experience. Black theologians, consciously or unconsciously following their white counterparts, often articulate the black experience in language that is meant to impress each other, not the persons about whom they speak. As long as this is so, Cone's assertion that "black theology is not academic theology" will be met with apathy and indifference.[2] So, instead of the existence of a necessary and unmistakable nexus between the black church and black theology, there seems to be a chasm between what black theology articulates and what the black church actually does. Theologians may postulate that black theology grows out of the black experience (including the black church), but the black church still feels isolated and distant. Somehow black theology has failed in its ability to reach the very people that it is designed to liberate. This is characteristic of the chasm that often exists between theory and practice, regardless of the discipline. However, if liberation methodologies have any chance of being institutionalized and implemented on a comprehensive level, the black church is the place to make this a reality.

James Cone's statement that black theology is not academic theology is more myth than reality because outside the halls of academia, black liberation theology seems to be more foreign to the black community than evangelical theology. How can it be anything other than academic if only the academicians are discussing it and writing about it? Black preachers tend to talk about evangelism, building programs, stewardship, and other practical theological and congregational issues. Unfortunately, black theology tends to be a concern only of academically oriented preachers. This certainly needs to change! As a method of analysis, a model of ministry, or simply a way of understanding life, black theology will have meaning and power when the masses of blacks begin to accept and practice it. This is not going to happen unless there is a conscious and systematic approach developed to gradually infuse the church with the concepts of liberation.

Some in the black church object to Cone's list of sources for black theology, which seems to include everything except the black church.[3] However, under his category labeled "Black History," he argues that black theology

> came into being when black churchmen realized that killing slave masters was doing the work of God. It began when black churchmen refused to accept the racist white church as consistent with the gospel of God. . . . The participation of the black churches in the black liberation struggle from the eighteenth to the twentieth century is a tribute to the endurance of black theology.[4]

Nevertheless, Cone fails to list the black church as a separate source of black theology and in effect relegates it to a subcomponent of black history. However, the black church is more than history—it is present and future. It is an intricate part of all the sources of black theology, such as experience, culture, scripture, revelation, and tradition. It was formed out of protest and the quest to be liberated in the midst of a society that was legally, morally, socially, economically, and politically oppressive. The black church needs to return to its protest posture, armed and ready to do battle, with the help of a new and creative ally—black theology.

Gayraud Wilmore, in his classic book *Black Religion and Black Radicalism*, lists three sources of black theology: the black community, the writings and addresses of black preachers and public men of the past, and the traditional religions of Africa. Although Wilmore mentions the black church, he does not expressly acknowledge in this particular context how important it has been to black theology. Wilmore states: "The theology of the black community is developed not in theological seminaries but on the streets, in the taverns and pool halls, as well as in the churches."[5] If there is any importance to the sequence of Wilmore's list, then we can only infer logically that the substance of black theology is developed more on the streets and in the taverns and pool halls than in seminaries, not to mention the black church. Wilmore, like Cone, seems to inadvertently relegate the church to a secondary status when discussing the development of theology. It is hard for me to believe that the theology of the black church is being developed on the streets of urban America where there is an abundance of disinterest in the value of life. Maybe this is not what Wilmore means; however, I have come to believe that there is little talk about God going on anywhere among black people except in churches and seminaries. Therefore, I beg to differ with these eminent theologians and submit that the church deserves a more prominent role in the shaping and perpetuation of black theology.[6] Although black theology has grown out of the experiences of black people, I would not place the church and other places such as the "streets and pool halls" on the same level in the development of a theological perspective.

Recently, Cone has focused more on the influence of the black church in his book, *For My People*. He asserts that black theology "is a theology of the black poor, reconstructing their hopes and God's coming liberated world."[7] I agree that black theology in any authentic form should grow out of the social, political, and spiritual experiences of the people in the churches and the community on a daily basis. It should be a theology developed in conjunction with those who actually live in poverty and experience disrespect and degradation. It should also be taught, preached, and advocated by those black pastors who labor with the masses. If every black preacher in cities, towns, and rural areas who pastors the poor and labors in the trenches where the stench of poverty and the despair of blacks are self-evident would begin to think of freedom in existential terms, then black liberation could be realized in a short time.

Black theology as liberation theology must be, according to Gustavo Gutierrez, the "theology of the people" if it is to affect the lives of people. Clearly the theological discourses of Gayraud Wilmore, J. Deotis Roberts, and James Cone have done much more to correct and offend the oppressor than the black church has done. The church seldom offends anyone. What Jens Glebe-Möller says about the Danish church can also be said about the black church in the United States: "It continues to contribute its mite to the legitimation of the status quo."[8] While it is justifiably argued that black liberation theology is experiential and biblical, it also appears to be more esoteric than pragmatic because black preachers shy away from the radical views of liberation theologians and side with traditional, conservative evangelical theologians, and black theologians have been unsuccessful in bringing their message to the church. This happens out of apathy and fear, or the inability to understand the concepts and ideas that will bring about liberation. While the actions of a few radical scholars and preachers have established the basis for liberation, a significant majority of black preachers and laypersons continue to be oblivious to the endemic nature of oppression and the need for a theology of liberation. Once this changes, freedom will have a chance to become reality.

What Is Black Theology?

Black theology is situational theology, as Allan Boesak asserts.[9] Like all theology, it is contextual. More importantly, it is indeed liberation theology, as some of its most articulate proponents—James Cone, Gayraud Wilmore, Albert Cleage, J. Deotis Roberts, and Major J. Jones—have eloquently argued.[10] It is also existential or contextual in that it is a theology of the black experience.

The most enduring and comprehensive definition of black theology was issued by the National Committee of Black Churchmen over two decades ago. Because of its importance, it is quoted here almost in its entirety.

> Black theology is a theology of black liberation. It seeks to plumb the black condition in the light of God's revelation in Jesus Christ, so that the black community can see that the gospel is commensurate with the achievement of black humanity. Black theology is a theology of "blackness." It is the affirmation of black humanity that emancipates black people from white racism, thus providing authentic freedom for both white and black people. It affirms the humanity of black people in that it says no to the encroachment of white oppression. The message of liberation is the revelation of God in the incarnation of Jesus Christ. Freedom is the gospel. Jesus is the liberator! The demand that Christ the Liberator imposes on all men requires all blacks to affirm their full dignity as persons and all whites to surrender their presumptions of superiority and abuses of power.[11]

Theological language and method are seldom in synchrony with the practices of the church. Clearly, the church is in need of a black practical theology whose function is to liberate it from the forces of social, political, and economic oppression. After understanding the nature of black theology, the critical question is, What does black theology do to bring about liberation and change in the lives of black and poor people? Certainly it purports that Jesus is the liberator and argues that God is on the side of the oppressed. How do these assertions, however hermeneutically sound and exegetically valid they may be, address the reality of poverty and suffering that is a direct result of the greed and selfishness our capitalist system perpetuates? How does black theology deal with the eradication of systemic oppression?

One of the problems confronting black theology is that it is not taught in black churches, state and national conventions, regional associations, ministers' conferences, or Christian education congresses. Ministers and pastors who are "doing theology" must begin to do liberation theology on a microcosmic scale, that is, within the local church. It is distressing that ministers and laypersons who participate in the church and other gatherings spend their time debating fruitless questions of internal authority and power, conforming to an evangelistic paradigm of the black church that is often patterned after Billy Graham, Robert Schuller, or other popular evangelists. The black church needs to free those within its ranks from the despair and powerlessness that grip their bodies and souls. Black theology provides the theoretical framework for this freedom.

Black Theology as Liberation Theology

James Cone is generally perceived as the leading systematic exponent of black theology.[12] Indeed, all of his major writings to date are variations on the liberation theme. Black theology believes that liberation is the essence of the gospel of Jesus Christ, and any authentic Christian theology affirms that God is on the side of the oppressed.

The theme of liberation is found throughout the Old Testament, but specifically in the book of Exodus and the prophets. The history of the Israelites' bondage in Egypt and their subsequent freedom, orchestrated by God, while Pharaoh's army drowned in the sea, is a critical corollary to the experience of blacks in America, except that pharaohs of modern history still oppress us. The exodus event shows Yahweh taking sides with the oppressed and fostering their liberation. As Boesak asserts, "This liberation message was the center and sustenance of the life of Israel."[13] James Cone made the point much earlier when he wrote, "The history of Israel is a history of God's election of a special, oppressed people to share in his creative involvement in the world on behalf of man."[14] Cone makes it clear that the church, in order to be authentic, has to participate in the activity of humanity liberation. He is essentially concerned with the liberation of blacks from systematic oppression, designed and orchestrated by whites, and the structure of the political and economic system.

Cone began to discuss the theme of liberation in his initial works, *Black Theology and Black Power* and *A Black Theology of Liberation*. However, he developed the concept of liberation more thoroughly in his later work, *God of the Oppressed*. He argues that "Jesus is the Ground of Liberation" and ties liberation to salvation.

Because human liberation is God's work of salvation in Jesus Christ, its source and meaning cannot be separated from Christology's sources (scripture, tradition, and social existence) and content (Jesus in his past, present, and future). Jesus Christ, therefore in his humanity and divinity, is the point of departure for a black theologian's analysis of the meaning of liberation. . . . Liberation is not an object but a "project" of freedom wherein the oppressed realize their fight for freedom is a divine right of creation. [15]

In Cone's view, liberation is the essence of Christianity and Jesus Christ is the liberator. Liberation manifests itself in the struggle for justice and freedom, and the black experience in the United States is the model of the struggle.

Moreover, Gayraud Wilmore correctly points out that black theology affirms the freedom of black people and negates that which seeks to deny them that freedom. He writes: "Black theology expresses both affirmation and negation. It affirms the real possibility of freedom and manhood for black people, and it negates every power that seeks to demand and rob black people of the determination of their own destiny." [16]

Black theology is self-affirmation with the understanding that God wills blacks to be free, equal, and at peace with themselves. In addition, black theology enables blacks to be free "from their traditional fear of whites, so that they not only can articulate their feelings but also so that they will act upon them." [17] The theme of self-respect and respect for all blacks is critical in black theology. Major J. Jones states:

Black theology holds that to be a person is to act like a person within any human context. This is the ultimate aim of Black theology. Black people must feel that they are completely capable and fit to live full lives under God and in relation to all God's children. . . . Black theology generates within black people the strength needed to resist the forces that threaten their humanity and that attempt to reduce them to an inhuman status less than that of a child of God. [18]

The critical point made by Jones is extremely significant because it suggests that black theology can enable blacks to stop victimizing each other—whether it be black-on-black crime or poor self-esteem. Black theology agrees with Jesse Jackson when he says, "I am somebody." This may seem small and obvious, but it is neither. It is very difficult for persons to believe in themselves if they have been historically downtrodden.

During the early years when black theology was in its embryonic stages, struggling to make itself known and felt in the hearts and minds of blacks and whites, Cone masterfully articulated the task and aim of black theology.

> The task of black theology then is to analyze the nature of the gospel of
> Jesus Christ in the light of oppressed black people so they will see the gospel
> as inseparable from their humiliated condition, bestowing on them the nec-
> essary power to break the chains of oppression. This means that it is a
> theology of and for the black community seeking to interpret the religious
> dimension of the forces of liberation in that community.[19]

If the gospel gives blacks the power to "break the chains" of oppression,
and black theology is the method of analyzing the gospel for that purpose,
then we need to move forward toward doing liberation. Black theologians
have articulated cogently a theology of liberation; however, these same
theologians along with the black church have fallen short in carrying it
out. The painful truth is that practicing liberation theology is much more
difficult than formulating it. But the formulation of it is a necessary pre-
condition to systematically effecting change through Christian practice.

Let me hasten to say that black theology is purported to have grown out
of the black community. In other words, it is a theology of the people,
coming out of the experiences of common folk. Cone and Wilmore make
this point quite eloquently in many of their writings.[20] The truth of their
assertion is basically unquestioned, but the principles of black theology
need to be applied seriously to the work of the ministry, that is, the function
of the church in the world today, if it is to be an effective agent of liberation
and change. Jones is adeptly correct when he states:

> Black theology has been and continues to be primarily a theology of pro-
> test. . . . Black theology calls for a more radical and complete revolutionary
> change. . . . Most current black theologians insist that to change the plight
> of blacks within the context of American culture will take nothing short of
> radical revolution. Whether or not such a revolution is violent is not the
> primary concern of many black theologians. Change alone is the concern.
> The call is for an unconditional commitment to change.[21]

Again, the call for change is one thing, but forcing change to occur is
quite another. The church, armed with black theology as a part of the
"armor of God," can begin to move beyond the rhetoric and semantics of
prophetic protest and begin to practice a theology of liberation. This is
where theory and practice converge and join hands to change the structure
of oppression and injustice in the United States and the world.

Black Theology as Holistic Ministry

Black liberation theology is the best available model to inform ministry in
the black church if the church is to be more than a clone of white evangelicalism. Black theology is concerned with the total person as well as

with the social structure in which we find ourselves. Roberts, in discussing the relationship of black theology and ministry, says:

> Our life in Christ, together with our worship and lifestyle, as individuals and as a people, should focus upon the improvement of our economic situation. Black theology is holistic—it does not see the well-being of the soul as unrelated to life in the body. Salvation includes the whole person and all of life. Sin and salvation are both personal and social. Evil and suffering are structural as well as personal. Against the background of such an understanding of the gospel, we must deal with the economic factor. Here is an essential contact point of black theology and ministry in the black church. [22]

Improving the economic situation will indeed hasten the day of our freedom. Too many blacks live from paycheck to paycheck while simultaneously trying to "keep up with the Joneses." The black church is, without question, an independent and generally financially solvent institution. But the individuals who constitute the church and community are often plagued by poverty on the one hand and inadequate financial planning and practice on the other. Those who are economically secure should translate their individual and personal success into the economic success of the black community without selling the community to the highest bidder or sacrificing the integrity of community unity and commitment to social progress.

Black theology can also inform our ministry with the poor, the sick, and the homeless. It teaches self respect and self-esteem in spite of the social and political reality that condescends to and oppresses blacks. Pastors need to empathize with the poor and develop ways to transform their status. This can start early with children and youth in order that they may aspire to become self-supporting individuals, committed to the betterment of church, community, and family. Indeed, black people have worked together to build some of the most beautiful, expansive and gloriously awesome church buildings that one could ever envision. Now is the time to harness that same creativity and commitment to deliberately and thoroughly make black liberation theology an intricate part of the everyday practice of ministry.

Black theology and practical theology should be two sides of the same coin. The practice of liberation theology is difficult because it begins with a hermeneutic that asks, How do I practice ministry according to the biblical text? What is the historical, social, and political context of the message that Jesus spoke according to the spokesmen for the early church? [23] In addition, we must ask, What does the Word of God mean to us as black people who are trapped in the seemingly inescapable web of socioeconomic and political disenfranchisement? These questions have to be specific because the interpretation or answers depends on who is asking and for what reason. White Western theologians and exegetes have historically interpreted the Scripture from an arrogant and dominant perspective because they represent the majority.

Hermeneutics is influenced by politics, experience, and culture. Black theology interprets the Scripture from a sociocultural perspective. White people have seen God through their privileged position, and, for a long time, blacks tried to use this same perspective. However, the development of black theology has taught blacks that their own experiences and culture are also important. More specifically, the black experience is uniquely akin to the experience of God's people as seen in the Bible. Therefore, blacks have come to understand God as seen through their own experiences of slavery, suffering, discrimination, and injustice.

Christianity for blacks has entailed a level of reality seldom visible to the dominant culture. Practicing Christianity has meant turning the other cheek, walking in humility, and enduring cruel and debased treatment as a social norm. Blacks learned how to sublimate their anger, and instead of destroying their chances for survival they learned how to live with the oppressors. This is real faith in the promise of God. This is why even today when we sing "There Is a Bright Side Somewhere," or "Climbing Up the Rough Side of the Mountain," everyone in the church is able to understand and identify with the words of suffering and hope, jubilation and reflection. Black theology endeavors to put in plain words the feelings, hopes, dreams, experiences, and practices of the black masses. These words used by black theology are girded by "the Word" of Scripture and the message of Jesus Christ.

Regretfully, some black churches have modeled themselves after the white church. Their worship services are characterized by brevity, quietness, anthems, and a general degree of formality. These blacks see this worship style as a form of sophistication that reflects compatibility with their educational level. However, I believe that black theology would wake these Christians up to the reality of their heritage, and help them to be proud of the struggles that their parents and foreparents endured for the sake of liberation. This pride would manifest itself in being unashamed to say "Amen" sometimes or even speak publicly about their difficult experiences. In this connection, I believe that Jesse Jackson pricked the conscience of black America when he referred to the "slop jar" and the "slave ship" in his nationally broadcast speech before the 1988 Democratic National Convention.[24] His heritage has shaped his ideology and his commitment to equity, fairness, and justice. Likewise, many blacks could identify with Jackson's experience because his experience is their experience. They too have lived with poverty and oppression.

Black professionals, that is, lawyers, doctors, professors, and so on, in a local area tend to attend the same Episcopal, Methodist, or Baptist church, thereby making these churches socioeconomically homogeneous. I am sure that in every city and town in America, there is a church within each major denomination that represents this paradigm. These enlightened, sophisticated, intelligent, successful blacks practice a European version of black religion. While black theologians highlight the uniqueness of black folk religion and the contributions of "Aunt Jane," these bourgeois blacks act as if they are trying to forget the days that Jesse Jackson chronicled and black theologians deem critical to our future. Some of these churches have no appreciation for gospel music, young people's choirs, innovative worship structures, or the use of other instruments in the worship setting except the organ and piano. This effort to imitate the oppressor holds these churches in bondage because they are unable to rejoice and weep with their other black brothers and sisters. Black theology will help them graduate from practicing religion as an exclusive experience of the head to understanding that it is also an experience of the heart. Until this is recognized, they too are not free. Cone reminds us that "liberation then is not merely a thought in my head; it is the socio-historical movement of a people from oppression to freedom—Israelites from Egypt and black people from American slavery."[25] Some blacks would do well to remember that their ancestors were also on those slave ships Jesse Jackson discussed. Blacks need to remember that neither education nor financial success cancels out our blackness. Whether we have a Ph.D., a D.D., or "no D at all," we are still black, and we possess a common heritage. The miseducation of blacks is still very much a part of our experience.

Black Theology in the Black Church

Black theology has little or no practical value apart from the black church; the liberation of black people cannot be achieved without the church's engagement of black theology. "Therefore, black liberation is, in part, dependent upon the attitude and role that the church assumes in relation to it."[26] Although some black preachers and theologians disagree as to the relationship of black theology to the church, the time for antagonism between preachers and theologians has passed. The urgency of achieving freedom and justice supersedes distrust and misunderstanding.

Black theology has rightly criticized the black church for being too otherworldly and conservative, and the church has been even harder on black theology by refusing to acknowledge it. The needed criticism of the church is what Cone calls "self-criticism," which started with a handful of progressive black ministers who saw the need for change. Now theology and ministry need to work together in order to bring about the freedom of our people. Black theology's rightful home is in the black church, and the black church needs to welcome black theology into the structure of its ministry. When this happens, liberation will be closer at hand.

Doing Liberation Theology: From Theory to Practice

There are several prevailing issues that face the church and society that must be addressed by pastors and church leaders. For example, sexism against black women should be addressed by black theology and the black church. Women in black churches outnumber men by more than two to one, but in positions of authority and responsibility the ratio is reversed. Although women are gradually entering ministry as bishops, pastors, deacons, and elders, many men and women still resist and fear that development. When the church where I formerly served as a pastor licensed a woman to the preaching ministry over a decade ago, almost all the male deacons and many women members opposed the action by appealing to tradition and selected Scripture passages. Black theology and the black church need to deal with the double bondage of black women in church and society.

There are two ways they can do so. The first is to treat black women with the same respect as men. This means that women who are qualified for ministry must be given the same opportunities as men to become pastors and to serve in such leadership positions as deacons, stewards, and trustees. Second, theology and the church must eliminate exclusionist language, attitudes, or practices, however benign or unintended, in order to benefit fully from the talents of women.

There are other ways that liberation theology can be practiced in the parish. Every black churchgoer, especially the economically secure, should understand that tithing or some larger form of proportionate giving significantly affects the liberation of blacks. A tithing church will be able to influence public policy issues such as housing for the poor and equal-employment opportunities. It would spend less time and energy raising money to meet the ordinary demands of ministry and mission, and actually *do* ministry by using its financial resources to develop ways to stem the tide of drug abuse, teenage pregnancy, divorce, and family violence.

Black churches can also adopt public schools, into which they can send volunteers to "testify" to young blacks about the value of a quality education. Churches could provide "education mentors" to work with teachers and counselors in order to help children increase educational achievement, develop self-esteem, and enhance moral and intellectual integrity. This would be the first step toward a decentralized educational structure that would enable communities and churches to take control of the future of our young people. In this scheme, churches would monitor the progress of their young parishioners from kindergarten through twelfth grade and find tutors or provide volunteers qualified to teach subjects in which children need help.

Black churches need to pool their financial resources by withdrawing funds from institutions that do not address the development needs of the black community. In our society, money talks. Black people should assume control of their hard-earned money and invest it in financial institutions that will challenge traditional models of risk management. Thus they will begin the process of nurturing our neglected communities back to health. The fiscal integrity of the black church and community depend on biblical and ethical principles such as working together, loving one another, and caring for the poor. In order for the black community to become a viable place for external investment, blacks will first have to invest in black youth and in the black community before society as a whole will invest in the black community.

Each black congregation should develop ways to assess the needs of its constituents and those who live within a certain radius of the church. This will enable the pastor and staff better to understand their ministry context and to address specific community needs. For example, some neighborhoods need to learn how to read, while others may need better access to medical care. Still others may simply need to know that there are people nearby who care about their families and are willing to offer a helping hand.

Black theology teaches self-respect and self-esteem in spite of social and political condescension to and oppression of blacks. Black pastors should put this into action by developing programs and policies to transform the status of the poor. They can do this by sharing historical and biographical stories of black accomplishments. Blacks have to regain the confidence that they can persevere despite modern manifestations of oppression and injustice. These lessons on determination, freedom, and faith can be correlated with biblical stories that express similar virtues.

As a pastor, I have historically invited young people to speak or read during the worship service. Moreover, I publicly acknowledge their educational accomplishments by recognizing the high achievers and encouraging others to strive toward excellence. This helps to develop their self-esteem, sense of achievement, and social skills. It also gives me an opportunity to work closely with those who may need to be motivated or encouraged. I have encouraged the church to provide opportunities for young people to develop leadership skills that can be transferred to other areas of life.

All of us are compelled to do more to bridge the gap between theory and practice. Black theology and the black church, working together, can potentially transform our communities. All of us have to hear anew the words of Scripture: "But be doers of the word, and not merely hearers who deceive themselves. . . . Those who look into the law of liberty, and persevere, being not hearers that forget but doers who act—they will be blessed in their doing" (James 1:22-25).

PART TWO

Pastoral Theology

4

Church
Administration

*The black minister is expected by the black church and the
black community to provide leadership, energy, and wisdom
in the struggle to change the oppressive economic, social, and
political burdens of black life in America.*
　　　　　　　　　　　　　—*Charles Shelby Rooks*

A s a theology of liberation, black theology is concerned with
understanding the Bible in light of the suffering and oppression of black people. God is viewed as a friend of the
poor—one who takes sides with the disenfranchised and despised. Jesus
is the norm, or the paradigm, of effectuating freedom whose mission was
and is to set the captive free. The Holy Spirit is the empowering force that
ultimately makes freedom possible.

Floyd Massey, Jr. and Samuel B. McKinney, in their book *Church
Administration in the Black Perspective*,[1] barely discuss the practice of
liberation as an administrative mandate. Church administration in the broad
sense is everything the church does from managing the budget, developing
tithing and stewardship theology, program planning, and office management
to preaching on Sunday morning. The saying that the preacher "does church
administration on Sunday morning from the pulpit," although true, needs
to be stated in a more comprehensive way in order to include the art and
practice of church administration.

Church Administration and Liberation

Black church administration is no longer a secondary issue. It is critical
to the development of a people who aspire to be free. Managing the church
in today's hostile social environment, which perpetuates inequality and
injustice, requires a commitment to liberation grounded in the belief that
God's divine plan does not include the subjugation of blacks. The church

71

needs a new focus and understanding of how it can help change the socio-economic and political position of blacks in the United States.

Church administration is not a series of disjointed decisions and actions but rather a systematic managing of goals, aspirations, objectives, potential, and power in the church. In the black church, it is a method of operating that will facilitate and enhance freedom and empowerment. C. Eric Lincoln is correct in saying, "Black religion is self-consciously committed to the destruction of caste in America and is moving quite visibly in some instances, less perceptibly in others, towards the principle that Christian commitment is inconsistent with powerlessness and lack of freedom."[2]

Black liberation theology not only correlates the experiences of Moses and the Israelites' bondage and captivity in Egypt with slavery in America, but also sets forth a new general principle of freedom as the apparent will of God. A theology of church administration grounded in the principles of black theology will empower and enable us to develop a management model that will facilitate the liberation struggle. Theology is the study of God as he relates to humanity. "Thus, 'theology comes from two Greek words,' we are told, *theos* meaning, 'God,' and *logos*, meaning word or 'rational thought.' "[3] A theology of church administration seeks to understand God and God's word in managing the work of the church in a way that frees and liberates it from the forces that perpetuate unfreedom. This theology seeks to empower those confronted by oppression and injustice with the intent of overcoming and surviving.

The experience of the black church has not been rosy. There are still many people who are systematically denied equality of results and access to that which can make life fairer and easier. The church has a mandate to be managed in a way that will facilitate the freedom of its people. This means that the theological framework should be based on an understanding of black liberation perspectives that will enable the living conditions of black and poor people to change for the better. Black theology is the sine qua non to establishing a practical program of freedom and liberation. The poverty, joblessness, illiteracy, and economic disparity that exist in the black community should not be accepted as the norm. A theology of church administration that seeks to transform this reality will bring about a cataclysmic change in the nature and structure of the black church community and the larger society. The church and community are intertwined, interconnected, and intermingled. In the words of Martin Luther King, Jr., the church and community are "tied together in a single garment of destiny."[4] Hiawatha Bray makes this clear when he says:

> There is a black church, for a common tradition of shared culture and shared oppression binds together all black congregations, distinguishing them from

their white counterparts. There is a unique style of black worship, and political concerns that are unique to black pastors and congregants. So important is the black church to black society that you cannot make sense of one without understanding the other.[5]

The relationship between the black church and the black community is also historically significant. "Thus, from the beginning, black people have associated Christianity with social and political freedom as well as spiritual salvation. They have not been as prone as white American Christians to speak of their faith in dichotomies such as soul versus body and political versus spiritual."[6] A black theology of church administration recognizes that the community is an extension of the black church, and its character and nature reflect the commitment extant in the church's efforts to transform it. This is why a new theology of church administration based on the teachings of liberation theology is necessary. The community still needs to be changed because the policies of the federal, state, and local governments have not significantly affected the status of blacks in America. A theology of church administration that accentuates political activism and encourages a new self-esteem and self-help needed to bring about change in the community is the first step toward liberation. The fact that the social condition of the black community is in need of repair should buttress the church's involvement. "Christian political activism grows out of the social condition of the community, conditions very different from those faced by whites. . . . Survival for blacks means . . . a battle for voting rights, jobs, better housing."[7]

In our modern post–Civil Rights society, the reality of the black condition has to be faced by the church in a way that will foster change. A systematic and thoroughgoing plan for transformation, once implemented, will change the status of the black community. This theology of administration confronts creatively external problems of poverty, unemployment, and racism. These problems have reached alarming proportions. Randall Frame states that

> poverty and unemployment rates for blacks are at their highest levels since the Civil Rights Act of 1964. In 1984, according to the Census Bureau, 34 out of every 100 black persons were living in poverty; and the black unemployment rate is near 15 percent—more than 40 percent among teenagers of working age. In 1984, the median black family had about 56 cents to spend for every one dollar for white families. And the infant mortality rate is about twice as high among blacks as whites.[8]

A meaningful liberation theology draws the church and community together in an effort to improve the condition of both. The church cannot afford to languish in eschatological hope. It must develop a plan to change the present reality based on commitment to the poor and disenfranchised. This commitment must result in actions that transform the economically anemic and politically obtuse condition of the black community.

A Christocentric Perspective

The Gospels tell the story of the experience of Jesus and the early Christians. However, Jesus is the major character in each, and his actions and teachings present a new and refreshing view of humanity and divinity. He preaches and teaches liberation and freedom (cf. Luke 4:16ff.). Jesus embodies the essence of love, compassion, caring, and sharing. He demonstrates the meaning of these virtues by example.

The Beatitudes capture the essence of Jesus' radical and liberating message to the multitudes—both then and now. Likewise, Jesus requires us to do good positively and that goodness is manifested in activities that reflect his life and character. Daniel Migliore states:

> When Christians confess that Jesus is a liberator, they are bearing witness that they have found in Him the concrete focus and goal of the liberation movement of God in the world. To receive by faith the spirit of the risen Jesus is to begin to live in the power of the radical freedom for God and for others that Jesus supremely actualized. Jesus liberated us for friendship and solidarity with others, especially with the despised and oppressed.[9]

In the United States, blacks constitute the largest part of the despised and oppressed community. The church is not exempt from the demeaning experiences of those who are outside the faith. This is why the nexus between the church and community is real. If the church is to be an agent of transformation, then it is called to relinquish any tendency toward isolationism or arrogant detachment and focus the gospel of Jesus Christ on helping those who are in need of spiritual direction and socioeconomic support.

> The Sermon on the Mount (cf. Matt. 5:1ff.) can be perceived as the New Testament corollary to the Old Testament Decalogue. Additionally, the Beatitudes are all promises of the kingdom of God, for to be in the Kingdom is to be comforted, to inherit the earth or the promised land, to be satisfied, to obtain mercy, to see God, and to be called his sons. They are also descriptions of those who receive the promises. Such people . . . although they are oppressed by the world, are merciful to others, and wherever they go, are the bringers and founders of peace. Jesus clearly expects his teachings to be put into practice. It is not a formless ethical ideal; and, although Paul and John are able to sum it up in the word "love," the Sermon on the Mount is concrete and specific.[10]

The commentator is correct in saying that Jesus intended his teachings to be put into practice. The poor in spirit, those who are hungry and thirsty for righteousness, the merciful, the pure in heart, the peacemakers, are all representatives of the kingdom of God.

A new liberation-oriented church administration seeks to understand and implement the teachings of Jesus as the model for transforming the community. This christocentric approach is guided by the character of Christ exemplified by his actions and passion for the oppressed, poor, and powerless. A black theology of church administration centers its policies in understanding the nature of Jesus in order that the programs of the church can reflect a new relationship between the church and community. This means that the church will have to reevaluate priorities and redirect some resources. The church needs to turn from the building fund or choir robes to spend more energy and money on eradicating poverty, crime, teenage pregnancy, and drug addition in the black community. A collective effort by pastors, laypersons, denominational leaders, and churches will transform the anemic status of the black community into a healthy, strong entity intent on changing the face of black America. "Black churches must do more things collectively. The individual operation serves its purpose, but can be served better when it is recognized that black people have far more compelling reasons to work, worship and strategize together than to stand apart."[11]

Collective strategy is crucial; however, the church needs to reassess its theological approach to the endemic problems that the black community faces. Historically there has not been a dichotomy between the black community and the black church, or the religious and the social. Today, however, there is a growing chasm between these two entities that is manifested in the church's continued focus on eschatology rather than on the contextual reality of injustice that keeps blacks unemployed, underemployed, and poorly paid. The church has a responsibility to its faith in Jesus to reflect a willingness to function as an agent of cataclysmic change. It needs to be willing to develop and administer programs and policies that reflect the spirit of Jesus' teachings exemplified in the Beatitudes. The German sociologist Max Weber incisively points out that the Sermon on the Mount deserves serious attention because it embodies the essence of the gospel.

> By the Sermon on the Mount, we mean that absolute ethic of the gospel, which is a more serious matter than those who are fond of quoting these commandments today believe. This ethic is no joking matter. The same holds for this ethic as has been said of causality in science: it is all or nothing. This is precisely the meaning of the gospel, if trivialities are not to result.[12]

The teachings of Jesus, in the Beatitudes (Matt. 5:1-2) and the Nazareth synagogue (Luke 4:18-1, Isa. 61:1-2), indicate that his message was radical and transformational. Since the church is to take seriously the message of Jesus Christ, it must look anew at the policies and practices that have little impact on transforming the social conditions that perpetuate and exacerbate inequities and oppression.

Christocentric church administration begins with Jesus as the paradigm for liberation and seeks to understand anew the Beatitudes as part of a theological framework designed to enable the development and implementation of church programs and activities that will transform the community. For example, some churches are involved in ministries that feed the hungry and clothe those in poverty. Christocentric church administration asks, What would Jesus do if confronted with this present reality? This forces the black church to face up to the awesome task of confronting the problems of poverty, peace, and brotherhood.

Blacks need to realize that they never will be rescued by external forces because these are the same forces that oppress. The black community can depend only on its own force or power to turn the tide of economic dependence, poverty, and social inequity. The church needs to join hands with the community in an effort based on self-determination, faith, planning, and unselfish pastoral leadership to change blacks' status as victims of poverty, powerlessness, and suffering in a land flowing with milk and honey.

Creativity in Pulpit and Pew

Creative leaders and followers are needed in ministry in the churches of urban America. The clergy and laity need to recommit themselves to eliminating the squalor and deprivation that exist in the black community. The entire church must understand that it has a stake in the future of blacks, and it can now begin to make plans toward shaping that future. Unless African Americans grab the reigns of their destiny with a new sense of commitment, their communities will implode and destroy themselves. Learning from experience, as reflected in the words of Joseph Washington, is critical and necessary for us to become stronger Christians.

> The black cult type, like black church and sect types is a creative, imaginative and indigenous (if insufficient) response to the failure of churches and society to satisfy the immediate needs of black people. These religious experiences are the acts of pride, dignity and self-reliance. All black religious responses intend this, some achieve it more successfully than others. Their primary aim is to end the ravages of inhumane treatment and posit a new reality.[13]

How do blacks end such ravages and begin to posit a new reality? I believe the answer lies in our understanding and approach to black theology. Operating the church within this specific theological framework lets the world know that we have a plan for altering the course of our community life. We will not achieve freedom and liberation unless the black church begins to develop systematically a means to upgrade the community. We have learned that the Civil Rights Act of 1964, the Great Society Programs of the Johnson administration, the War on Poverty, the New Federalism, Urban Renewal and Revitalization, and a potpourri of other programs have not achieved equality, fairness, and economic independence for black Americans. Clearly, the status of blacks is ultimately tied to the creativity and commitment of the church. A black theology of church administration thus is crucial. It will redirect our energy and resources in order to change the social conditions of millions of black people who are victimized by a vicious cycle of miseducation and poverty.

Though black theology is no longer new, it is in fact new to the church. Black ministers need to be creative and innovative in incorporating the ideas and concepts of liberation into sermons, midweek worship services, seminars, workshops, and program activities. Children and young people need to be taught the importance of black pride along with the historical contributions that blacks have already made toward the liberation struggle.

Here is an example of creativity in the church. Several local churches could combine resources and sponsor interchurch seminars on liberation theology, bringing in leading black American and African theologians to teach and discuss strategies for a week. Most black churches hold annual revivals. There is also a need for an annual symposium on black theology held for ministers and laypersons in the context of the church. There is no limit to the creative talent within the hearts and minds of black clergy and laity. We need to use the talents that God has given us to chart a new course for the church and the black community.

The Black Church and the Poor

The numbers of black poor are increasing at an alarming rate, and there is reason for the church to be extremely concerned. A decade ago, James Cone wrote, "As a rule, the church's behavior toward the poor is very similar to the society at large: The poor are charity cases."[14] Unfortunately, Cone is correct because the black church has taken on the air of mainstream America and emulated the snobbery and disinterest in the welfare of the poor that is perpetuated by the wielders of power and money. In various forums I have been confronted with the assertion by theologians, pastors, and laity that the black church is becoming more and more a middle-class institution, oblivious to the needs and concerns of the poor. While I do not have a socioeconomic profile of black churchgoers that can be generalized, my own limited sample in an earlier study certainly confirmed the validity of this assertion.[15]

Although the black church may be somewhat removed from the experience of abject poverty, it still has a responsibility to understand the poverty issue and to develop a method and program for combating it. Because the church is socially homogeneous, and most people want to look their best, dress their best, and generally reflect and compete with each other, it is quite difficult to ascertain, through observation or survey research, what the reality is. Even the poorest of individuals often look prosperous on Sunday morning. For example, I remember that when I was a child, I looked as good as anyone else for church, but we were dirt-poor. A family of twelve with one parent working outside the home could hardly be characterized otherwise. However, we were blessed and spiritually rich. The words of Scripture, "I know your affliction and your poverty, even though you are rich" (Rev. 2:9), enabled us to keep on keeping on.

The black church looks more middle class than it actually is. It can be more accurately characterized as a conglomerate of working people in low- to moderate-paying jobs. Sar Levitan and Isaac Shapiro call these people the working poor.[16] However, it is logical to hypothesize that the black church population is more middle class than the general black population.

In the article "America's Hidden Poor," the writer states: "Most working poor, unlike a hard-core group of inner-city welfare mothers, don't remain mired in poverty for a decade or more at a time. Thus, the bulk of Americans who plug away at a job year after year still get ahead. But the working poor are also at the mercy of larger economic trends . . ."[17] Black people are less likely than whites to be working at all, and while the working poor are mostly white, many blacks are either not working or struggling to find work.[18]

Moreover, the percentage of the black population not working at any given time is generally higher than that of whites. Poverty is real for most black people—now or regularly in the past. Black liberation theology enables the poor to possess a sense of dignity and hope by reminding them that God is on their side. The church is responsible for teaching blacks that poverty is a direct result of the greedy, oppressive nature and policies of a society that puts personal gain ahead of community needs. In some cases, it is the result of misguided values and poor work habits, but for the most part, it is directly related to the economic system.

The black church cannot ignore the question of poverty. Michael Harrington, in his book *The New American Poverty*, says: "In 1980 when Ronald Reagan launched his savage assault upon the welfare state, there was little effective protest as the poor suffered cuts in government spending two and a half times greater than were received by all the other groups combined.[19] Government has never really been seriously concerned about the poor or the eradication of poverty. In a capitalist system, the concern is more with individual profits and prosperity than with poverty and oppression. The myth of believing otherwise is unfortunate. Harrington exposes the illusion when he states: "There never was a gigantic program of handouts to the poor, and to the minority poor in particular, called the War on Poverty. . . . There never was a massive investment of billions of dollars in radical innovations that challenged the very structure of power in the United States."[20]

The church has to be innovative and confront those who perpetuate the myths, and teach black people how to help each other. Those who are prosperous have an even greater responsibility to the poor and needy. They need to be in solidarity with their brothers and sisters in the same way that Job was committed to those in need:

> Because I delivered the poor who cried, and the orphan who had no helper. The blessing of the wretched came upon me, and I caused the widow's heart to sing for joy. I put on righteousness, and it clothed me; my justice was like a robe and a turban. I was eyes to the blind, and feet to the lame. I was a father to the needy, and I championed the cause of the stranger.
>
> (Job 29:12-16)

Commitment to the poor is found throughout biblical literature. "Those who mock the poor insult their Maker" (Prov. 17:5). Helping the poor is a part of the justice and righteousness of God, and the black church, often a victim of apathy and co-optation, needs to rethink its position on the poor. Jesus was a friend to the poor. Likewise, we want it said of our deeds: "For I was hungry and you gave me food, I was thirsty and you gave me something to drink, I was a stranger and you welcomed me, I was naked and you gave me clothing, I was sick and you took care of me, I was in prison and you visited me" (Matt. 25:35-36). Because some of our churches have very few persons who could be called poor by the standards of poverty that exist in some Third World countries, it is very important for us to understand the nature of poverty and the extent to which most of us in American churches are not poor.

The Black Church's Economic Strength

The black church is the most significant and powerful institution in the black community, but its power has been diluted by its failure to recognize its economic strength. No other black organization can claim the economic power that is inherent in the black church.

However, every Monday morning in cities, towns, and villages throughout America, from New York to California, black churches deposit millions of dollars in banks owned and operated by whites. These banks in turn use this money to invest in whatever is profitable, whether in Latin America or South Africa. The black church is in effect subsidizing the demise of its own people. It is funding the oppression of the black community by building up the coffers of those who control the economic, political, and social structure. Furthermore, the church is naively and inadvertently in complicity with the forces of power—forces that mastermind and sustain a double standard in the United States and throughout the world. Where the church places its money reflects its commitment to the liberation struggle.

The black church has often been accused of being too preoccupied with other-worldly aspirations to realize that much can be done in this world to change the condition of the black community. But we seem to be unwilling to confront the wielders of power and prestige who essentially are the architects of injustice. The spirit of protest and prophecy has been thwarted by the comfort of individual position and the desire to be a king or kingmaker in church, community, and nation. The attitude and vision of the biblical prophets such as Isaiah, Amos, or Jeremiah are no longer evident in the black church.

Many have heard the expression "money talks," and money is obviously a powerful medium. Nevertheless, the church has failed to understand its own economic strength—a strength capable of fostering liberation and social change if properly managed and understood. One way to change how blacks are treated is for local churches in every city, town, and rural community to withdraw every dollar from the white-controlled banks and place their money in a black institution sensitive or responsive to the needs of the poor and minorities. Black banks governed by policies that are oppressive, self-centered, and fostered by greed must be treated as if they too were white-owned and controlled because if they treat people like whites do, then they too are oppressive.

A more innovative approach to economic liberation would involve black churches forming their own banks by pooling their capital resources and developing regional banking facilities to meet the needs of the people. Also, there is a serious need for some of the small, poorly organized churches to consolidate their resources and merge with each other. This would reduce the fixed costs and operating costs, thereby allowing for more meaningful ministry. Instead of having several churches in one community with only a few members each, a community could have one church, one pastor, one mortgage with several hundred members.

The Pastor As Leader

Although we live in an age in which pastors have been relegated to being only spiritual leaders, the black church cannot be totally effective without the support and involvement of the pastor in all areas of its life. The minister is more than the "spiritual leader" in the church. He or she is the leader, spiritual and administrative. There is no theological basis for dichotomizing the work of the ministry into spiritual and secular realms.

While some pastors have abdicated their responsibility, others have been kept from fulfilling their task by churches that refuse to allow the pastor to use his or her leadership gifts. This is unfortunate and indicative of the prevailing attitude in some churches that the pastor is a hired servant who does only what parishioners want. While the pastor needs to work with laypersons in guiding their Christian development, he or she also needs to provide leadership. This does not mean that others cannot do some things—but the pastor has to choose persons who will help in leading the church to do God's will (cf. Exod. 18:13-27). The Bible does not indicate that churches need trustees; however, there is a legal need for them in most states and municipalities. The church needs to develop qualifications for trustees that are biblically based. Moreover, I believe that the board status of trustees, coupled with the fact that the church has often used a different set of rules for selecting them, has caused the black church a great deal of internal stress. Trustees must be "full of the spirit and of wisdom" and have the same qualifications as deacons (cf. Acts 6:1-7; 1 Tim. 3:8-13). Instead of being custodians of the church's property, that is, maintaining it, they have often acted as owners and policymakers—a task that belongs to all of the people and the pastor of the flock.

The black pastor must regain his or her position as the leader of the church. The minister is called to pastor a church in order that he or she can lead God's people, not to follow the boards or the people. The minister has the responsibility to "Proclaim the message whether the time is favorable or unfavorable" (2 Tim. 4:2). The pastor who understands his or her position and responsibility will become the leader of the church. This is not the same as a dictator, an overused term to describe a strong pastor. The pastor as leader will delegate and share responsibility. However, he or she cannot abdicate his or her responsibility and call to lead God's people.

The multi-staff black church is the wave of the future. Single-person leadership has lost its attractiveness to pastors who are secure in their ministry and understand the old saying that "two heads are better than one." A large church also will work one person to death, so necessity often demands staff development and expansion. The pastor also needs to spend time in self-development that includes relaxation, family activities, and continuing education in order to remain fresh in his or her thinking and invigorated and excited in the practice of ministry.

The staff—assistant and associate pastors, minister of music, Christian education director, church secretary, custodians—all fall under the supervision and responsibility of the pastor. Regular staff meetings will help prevent problems and enable the smooth planning of other activities that will help to make the church a more effective institution.

The pastor also has a critical role in the development of the budget and in the entire budget process. As administrative leader, he or she needs to have veto power, appointive power, and the authority to determine how funds are raised and disbursed. The astute pastor does not want to handle the money; indeed, he or she should not because it is the source of too much temptation and controversy. However, the pastor needs to be a key player in constructing monetary or financial policy. Again, this does not mean that the pastor should be a unilateral decision maker consulting no one. But it does mean that a strong pastor, with developed leadership skills, must be decisive, self-assured, and willing to take calculated risks. He or she needs the support of the people and needs to lead the congregation without falling into the trap of following those whom God has called him or her to lead.

Although we all need and want to be liked by others, the pastor is not in a popularity contest. He or she works for justice and righteousness, and some traditions will change, some persons may leave their positions, and liberation theory and practices will become a part of the new order in the black church. For the pastor to lead the church, he or she must be well educated in theology and other areas that will make him or her a competent decision maker. The pastor should read everything available and be thoroughly versed in black studies and biblical studies.

Management Theories

Several theories of management used in business and government will enhance the pastor's management skills. Like other organizations, the church consists of people. The pastor's skill in communicating with the church people is more critical to effective ministry than any other attribute. However, unlike some major business organizations, the church uses very little technology. To be sure, computers are used to organize church records and produce reports, but, for the most part, the church is a people organization. It is saturated with those who have come to "hear a word from the Lord," and to be motivated to live spiritually enriching lives. However, people who come to church and support its many levels and areas of ministry also expect the pastor to be well informed and skilled in the overall operations of the church. Today, as in the past, a basic prerequisite for serving the church is that the pastor has to be an excellent and exciting preacher; however, the pastor also needs to be skilled in management theory and practice. The ability to motivate laypersons to do the work of the ministry in an effective, cooperative, and Christ-like manner is critical. This is no small task in the church because personalities, families, traditions, and other factors can often hinder the work of ministry.

Theory Z

Theory Z is based on the Japanese model of managing productivity. William Ouchi, credited with developing the term, explains the theory by saying, "Quite simply, it suggests that involved workers are the key to increased productivity."[21] In the church, the effort to get people "involved" is critical to program planning and development or ministry enhancement. Pastors often lament the lack of involvement of so many churchgoers. For example, pastors tend to respond to questions regarding the numerical size of their churches in ideal terms. But when pragmatism overcomes this idealism, the size of the church is generally reduced considerably. The task of the pastor is to encourage and motivate churchgoers to become involved. Otherwise, the pastor will be doing the work of the laity. In other words, the pastor's failure to involve others will result in him or her being overworked and distressed. People need to feel that the minister wants them to be involved, and that they should do the best they can to produce meaningful ideas, plans, and activities.

This is especially important when one takes on a new pastorate. One of my mentors, Dr. Samuel Proctor, says that getting large numbers of persons involved in developing ministry strategies, such as program planning, evaluating the current status of the church in areas like finances, Christian education and worship, missions and social concerns will help to build strong relationships with those who voted for and against you as the new leader. Coupled with strong preaching and visiting the sick, this will help the new pastor get started on a strong foundation.[22]

Theory Z states that the first lesson to be learned is trust. Productivity and trust go together.[23] Well, trust is a standard Christian virtue. Churchgoers oftentimes preach, sing, testify, and pray about trust. Trust is not only a corollary to productivity, but goes hand in hand with love, commitment, sacrifice, hope, joy and obedience. Blacks are used to singing "I will trust in the lord . . . until I die," and "Trust and obey, for there is no other way . . ." Trust in each other is very important for church growth, maximizing budget potential, and learning more about the word of God as it manifests itself in the lives of the faithful.

Nevertheless, a lack of trust grips the church either because persons have been betrayed by church leaders or by pastors who have conformed to some of the negative images that H. Beecher Hicks describes in his book *Images of the Black Preacher*.[24] However, the pastor has the responsibility of restoring and engendering trust. Parishioners are to trust the pastor and each other. This is an ingredient of true Christianity. Conversely, distrust breeds hostility and social upheaval. In the black church distrust results in poor participation within and among auxiliaries, feuds between deacons, trustees, and pastor, and hostile attitudes during church business meetings. Distrust also results in the lack of fellowship among ministers and churches.

Theory Z also teaches the minister how to be subtle or deftly ingenious. "Relationships between people are always complex and changing. A foreman who knows his workers well can pinpoint personalities, decide who works well with whom, and thus put together work teams of maximal effectiveness."[25] Likewise, the minister who knows how to use subtlety to appoint committees for program planning and other church functions and activities will be saved a lot of unnecessary trouble. Some people do not have the right personality to usher or work effectively with others. Some churchgoers have mean, ugly, disruptive attitudes. Others like to be in charge. Still others are cooperative, kind, and loving. The pastor has to know and understand each person and work effectively with all. Effective ministry depends on good management skills and decisions as well as prayer and commitment to God's word. More precisely, the pastor is not only an evangelist, counselor, teacher, and friend, but also a manager who loves people. The pastor knows through experience that it's better to put people who work well together on the same committee if he or she wants the work to get done. Asking for volunteers to serve on some commissions or groups is often a poor management decision and can lead to the demise of the project, a regressive outcome.

Finally, theory Z emphasizes consensus, teamwork, and participation. It puts everyone on an equal plane. The church that treats everyone equally, regardless of social status, family background, years of affiliation, or gender, will be a progressive and forward-moving organization. Moreover, if the pastor and laity trust each other to be responsible, fair, and equal, then the black church will be free to minister to those who are oppressed within and without.

Theory X and Theory Y

These two theories of motivation have been discussed and applied to church management more than others. Accordingly, they are reviewed briefly here.

Douglas McGregor has argued that managers function and operate based upon underlying assumptions about the nature of people.[26] These assumptions were called theory X and theory Y.

The manager who embraces theory X assumes that people are by nature lazy and irresponsible and must be monitored constantly. Theory X managers have been said to think of people as jackasses who basically have to be pushed along. On the other hand, theory Y assumes that people are basically responsible and hardworking, and simply need to be encouraged in their work.[27]

The minister who embraces the theory X model of managing assumes that people have to be told what to do after being given certain tasks, and that they cannot be trusted to do what they have been asked, so they must be watched constantly. Such a pastor feels that people do a good job because of the promise of reward or punishment. Some persons do have to be told what to do, especially if they have not experienced ongoing training, Bible study, workshops, or seminars on faith development. Needless to say, however, the pastor should refrain from using the theory X model because it does not reflect the spirit of Christ. Conversely, the pastor whose management style is based upon theory Y will be supportive and encouraging, positively reinforcing the good intentions that those who love the Lord possess. Theory Y is certainly more akin to what the church espouses, and it represents the spirit of Christianity and approach to management that we find in theory Z.

Organization Development

Organization development (OD) is a relatively new management strategy that assumes that most organizations need to change. It emphasizes the process of human interaction and views the organization as a social system.[28] The black church is without question a social organization, as has been noted by psychologists and theologians. Organizational development theorists feel that "organizations must become more adaptable, flexible and innovative to survive."[29] Applied to the black church, this approach would prevent the church from becoming static and captive to tradition.

Organizational development theory assumes that people want to be supported, trusted, and cooperative. David R. Morgan, in his book *Managing Urban America*, lists the following steps of an OD effort:

> Problem Recognition
> Data Gathering
> Diagnosis
> Feedback to Management
> Intervention

Assessment of Progress
Continuation of the Program[30]

Outside consultants or change agents are often brought into the organization to apply the tenets of OD. Since the pastor is more often than not perceived as an outsider and a change agent, he or she is in a good position to implement OD. For example, a church may suffer from poor church school attendance. It is a problem that is easily recognized; however, the intervention stage may reveal that poor attendance continues after repeated calls for greater participation. Further analysis may reveal, for example, that lack of transportation is the reason for poor attendance. An intervention tactic that solved the problem would enhance church school development.

Understanding the nature and value of organization development theory will help the pastor manage the church in a way that will help it adjust to the needs of the community. Thus the pastor, laity, and community move a step closer toward the goal of liberation.

Conflict Management

Conflict in the church is exacerbated by social conflict in the structure of society. Pastor and people do not always have the same vision, expectations, or understanding of issues. Simply stated, a conflict arises when two or more persons are unable to see eye to eye. The subject of conflict ranges from deciding the color of choir robes or some other uniform to voting to call or dismiss a pastor. If there is no consensus of opinion or resolve, a situation is ripe for conflict.

While some ministers seem to thrive on conflict, most are eager to develop ways to regulate it. Conflict cannot be avoided totally because the cost of progress may be conflict with some individual or organization. The successful pastor uses scriptural teaching, compassionate understanding, and the love of people, along with management theories to minimize conflict within the black church.

One of the best books on the subject of conflict theory is *Conflict Regulation* by Paul Wehr.[31] He provides a detailed analysis of conflict and suggests several models of conflict regulation. Although the focus is on social and geopolitical systems, I have found that the theory can be creatively applied to managing conflict within the church. Two models for understanding, regulating, and resolving conflict in the church are what I term the Gandhian model and the Jesus model. The essence of both models is based on agape.

The Gandhian Model

Mahatma Gandhi, the Indian philosopher, developed a model of self-limiting conflict that has been used by Martin Luther King, Jr. and Cesar Chavez in the United States. Their social movements, namely, for equal rights, benefited from the adaptation of Gandhi's model to the plight of blacks and poor in an effort to achieve liberation. A prominent feature of this model is the "Step-wise Strategy": a series of steps, each more difficult than the preceding one, used to resolve or regulate conflict. This process begins with negotiation and arbitration. "At this preliminary state [Gandhi] established the close, cooperative, personal relationship with opponents that would later limit the antagonism normally generated by the escalation process."[32] If the conflict was not resolved at this step, the satyagraha would prepare for direct action and proceed to more advanced steps such as agitation, ultimatum, and noncooperation. Because the Gandhian model has several phases, it limits the severity of confrontation and conflict while simultaneously leading to a new understanding of truth.[33]

In this model of self-limiting conflict, nonviolence or *ahimsa* is the key ingredient. Each participant has to be committed to nonviolent action. However, nonviolence sometimes evokes violent responses from others. This reaction was seen quite frequently during the Civil Rights movement led by Martin Luther King, Jr.

Now, how is this model helpful to the church? Can the principles be transferred to conflicts that arise among individuals and groups in the church? I think the answer is yes. For example, this model can be used in marriage counseling. The pastor is often asked to counsel couples who are experiencing conflict—especially conflict that has led to spousal abuse. This model is based on a nonviolent step-by-step approach to conflict resolution, and each step leads closer to the ideal of truth. Marriage is based on honesty, mutual respect, and the value of truthfulness. Moreover, "the Gandhian model of conflict-waging inhibits the conflict personalization process. It reduces threat by stressing the maintenance of good personal relations with opponents while pressing the issues."[34]

This model can be used to teach churchgoers how to become issue-oriented and not commit the fallacy of *argumentum ad hominen*, which is to switch the argument from the issue to the individual. This is often done in the church when personalities clash and emotion is more prominent than intellect.

The Gandhian model of regulating conflict reminds me of the spirit and posture of Jesus, who encourages us to love our enemies and do good to those who hate us.

The Jesus Model

The church, though founded on this model, often fails in its practice of peace because we allow conflicts to simmer and escalate into full-blown internal battles. The Jesus model, nonviolent like the Gandhian model, can be summed up in the words the writer of Luke's gospel attributes to Jesus during his Sermon on the Plain.

> But I say to you that listen, *Love your enemies*, do good to those who hate you, bless those who curse you, pray for those who abuse you. *If anyone strikes you on the cheek, offer the other also*; and anyone who takes away your coat do not withhold even your shirt. Give to everyone who begs from you; and if anyone takes away your goods, do not ask for them again. Do to others as you would have them do to you.
>
> (Luke 6:27-31)

Conflict among blacks is fueled by their social and political dilemma, that is, the lack of respect and other difficulties they face in the larger society. Some black professionals believe that because they are successful educators or entrepreneurs, they are likewise qualified to run the church. In addition, there is a growing number of laypersons who are so well trained in their fields that their secular training and education may exceed that of the pastor. While this does not mean that they are more qualified than the pastor, their input and ideas may serve to advance the gospel of Jesus Christ. As the black church becomes more educated and complex, the potential for internal conflict becomes greater. The authority of the pastor is more subject to challenge and debate. However, the pastor with a thorough understanding of the word of God, augmented by a positive understanding of self, will be able to lead, listen to others, and help the church move beyond discord and self-destruction to a new level of liberation.

Jesus' admonition to love our enemies is difficult for us, but our faith enables us to believe that love is indeed a more powerful force than hate, and peace is a more noble goal than conflict. Jesus says, "If any want to become my followers, let them deny themselves and take up their cross daily and follow me" (Luke 9:23). Following him is the most ethical and morally right way to manage conflict in the church.

5

Worship and Preaching

I was glad when they said to me, "Let us go into the house of the Lord!"

—*Psalm 122:1*

Worship, therefore, is not primarily an expression of the individual's private relationship with God. It is rather a community happening, an eschatological invasion of God into the gathered community of victims, empowering them with the divine spirit from on high, to keep on keeping on even though the odds might appear to be against them. In the collective presence of the poor at worship, God re-creates them as a liberated community.

—*James H. Cone,*
For My People

Every Sunday morning throughout America—from small towns in Virginia to the large urban areas of New York, Detroit, and Los Angeles—millions of African Americans gather in churches to worship. Most are Baptist, Methodist, and Pentecostals because these constitute the largest organized groups of blacks in the United States. That these people are convoked in their individual places of worship suggests both the meaningfulness of religious experience in the local church and the social implications of black worship. Moreover, worship as a shared experience in the black church is a set of emotions and personal experiences that converge on Sunday morning. These emotions and experiences are related to the church and the world—to a life often filled with trials and tribulation.

Black America, however, exists in a world quite different from the racially and culturally homogeneous church. Historically, worship has enabled black people to cope with oppression and racism. Individuals who were nobody in society became somebody in church. The church provided, and continues to provide, the support needed to assure people that they are valuable. While worship in the black tradition needs to provide the self-enhancing mechanism for individual coping, it can be even more significant when also made to be a means for social change. Worship is generally designed to bring about spiritual change in the individual. Too often, however, passive acquiescence to the social order continues. Rather, the status quo should be confronted with the boldness of Jesus, Peter, and John.

Worship should be oriented toward transformation—both spiritual and social. True spiritual transformation enables one to treat others right and endeavors to change society so that justice and fairness become the norm. Authentic spiritual transformation, therefore, leads to social transformation. Paul, writing to the Romans, says, "Do not be conformed to this world, but be transformed by the renewing of your minds, so that you may discern what is the will of God—good and acceptable and perfect" (Rom. 12:2). Inasmuch as black worship purports to be Christ centered, it must demonstrate what Paul meant when he demanded that we become new creations—that a new outlook be understood, accepted, and practiced.

This new creation includes a new social order, which cannot be realized if our worship services do not provide people with the desire for change and the means for redirecting their lives, which are hampered by injustice. Blacks are victimized by discrimination, poverty, joblessness, poor self-esteem, and a host of other atrocities. These are moral and ethical problems with which religion and worship should deal. Simply stated, it is not only irrational, but ethically unjust for people to be gripped by despair in a land flowing with milk and honey. Moreover, to accept this condition and engage in worship that is almost exclusively oriented toward the afterlife is itself callous and oppressive. The black church cannot afford this type of eschatological hoopla masquerading as worship of the God of love, mercy, and justice. James Cone, in his book *Speaking the Truth*, poignantly speaks of black worship: "During the worship service, God is known by the immediate presence of the divine spirit with the people, giving them not only the vision that the society must be transformed but also the power and courage to participate in its transformation."[1]

Justice and Righteousness in Worship

The prophet Amos is eloquent in explaining authentic worship and preaching. He writes, "Take away from me the noise of your songs; I will not listen to the melody of your harps. But let justice roll down like waters, and righteousness like an everflowing stream" (Amos 5:23-24). Justice and righteousness constitute the heart of the prophet's preaching, and in order for black preachers to make a difference in the condition of life in America, their message needs to be laden with themes of freedom and justice. However, many black preachers today are following the white evangelical model of preaching redemption from personal sin, while ignoring the fact that people need to be "saved" from political and economic oppression and injustice.

The church must be about freedom and justice if it is to be about the word of God. The prophet Amos became very upset and prophesied against the people of God precisely because of their apathy toward the poor, the suffering, and the needy, while the Israelites languished in their rituals and form. God is not concerned with style and form. The style and form of worship and preaching are intended to please people and not God. The substance of worship pleases God. If worship is filled with music that pleases the ear and a sermon that causes shouts and widespread jubilation without addressing the existential situation of most black people, then worship has failed to address a significant part of the human condition.

Like the prophet Amos, the black preacher as worship leader is concerned with the absence of justice and righteousness in his or her community and church. Worship, apart from addressing issues of fairness and goodness, is nothing more than a meaningless exercise in expedience and self-indulgence that does not please God. We need to recapture the spirit of prophecy that gripped biblical leaders such as Amos, Jeremiah, and Isaiah, and compelled them to speak harshly to a people who felt they were doing well and should be applauded for their support of the temple shrines and the status quo.

We do not expect white preachers to confront the status quo in their sermons and lectures; however, it appears that black preachers are unwilling and afraid to prophesy against the injustice and unrighteousness endemic to modern society. Surely this is not a new phenomenon inasmuch as the black church has, to a large extent, been a conservative institution on social and political issues. Although it has also been the most important institution in the black community, it has failed to bring about a massive, thoroughgoing change in the condition of black life in America. This is exactly what can be accomplished if we channel the effort to foster change through the church. Certainly this will mean that a deliberate effort to change the perception of worship and its ingredients must be made.

Worship, when understood as an integral part of life, will not be divorced from the fact that blacks are oppressed and sometimes oppressive toward each other: teenage pregnancy has reached epidemic proportions in the black community; joblessness and poverty are facts of life; racism and invidious discrimination are rampant although more covert than in the days of Jim Crow; and black-on-black crime continues to figure heavily in the statistics on death and violent street crime in America. Neither the preacher nor the church is unaware of this reality; however, there is a deafening silence in the churches concerning these social problems. We ask: Is the church guilty of "blaming the victims," as William Ryan has so eloquently asserted in his book by the same title?[2] Has the black church become immune to the problems that beset the black community?

Preachers need to address these problems by preaching systematically about the need for justice, respect for others and oneself, and the importance of doing God's will. Some will object to this emphasis because there has been a tendency to separate the spiritual or religious from the social and political. However, several years ago, Kenneth Clark, a social psychologist and critic of the church, described the black church as a social institution.[3] It is clearly that; however, I am suggesting that it deliberately become more political by addressing some of the tough social and political problems in the context of worship. The pastor will have to lead this effort by becoming adept at making the correlation between prophetic preaching and liberation within the community.

The prophet Amos wrote other searing and indicting words, "I hate, I despise your festivals, and I take no delight in your solemn assemblies" (5:21). Likewise, God is not pleased with our Sunday gatherings unless they reflect a love of justice and righteousness. This means that worship in black churches has to be more than jubilant celebration. The new worship experience will begin to bring about justice and righteousness in the church and in society, thereby enabling the black church to become a force to be reckoned with by the rulers of this world.

Worship as Transformation

As a pastor, I have asserted that the church is a change agent; however, it is more than that. Because the church is equipped with the gospel of Jesus Christ, it has the power to transform lives. Individual and community transformation is the end result of worship. Those who worship God week after week should not display the same actions and behavior as those who do not. Their perspective and attitude should change, and they should also be able to help change others. Paul says, "Be not conformed . . . but be ye transformed. . . ." Transformation implies conversion and apparent change. Conversion should manifest itself by making us different spiritually, socially, and politically. This will mean that our conversion or transformation, springing forth from the structured worship in the church, will become the basis of our efforts to transform society into a more egalitarian community where justice and righteousness will be more reality than myth.

Conversion, to be born again, or to receive salvation is a process of becoming more attuned to understanding the meaning of the kingdom of God here and now. When we become saved, we will understand that social and political justice are intimately connected to salvation and a born-again status. Individual salvation has as a necessary correlate the salvation of the community. Worship properly understood and practiced facilitates the salvation of both. Inasmuch as the black community is victimized by so many internal and external injustices, it needs to be saved. However, as long as we think of salvation as an individual, personal experience, instead of a community experience, we fail to understand the Exodus event as a paradigm, not only of liberation, but also of salvation. Contrary to what blacks were taught during slavery, salvation apart from liberation is inconsistent with the gospel message. To be "saved" is to be a new creation, and a new creation implies complete transformation.

Joyful Noise in Worship

Worship in the black church is more often than not a joyful experience. It is joyful because blacks experience a sense of freedom seldom felt in the everyday struggles of dealing with racism and various forms of injustice. One is free to be himself or herself because the church experience fosters a kindred spirit that enables "everybody to be somebody." In authentic worship there is a bond of unity that makes "Aunt Jane" and "Doctor so-and-so" brothers and sisters. Education and socioeconomic status are superceded by faith in a loving God. The worship environment fosters spiritual and emotional freedom. It presents one with the opportunity to cry, sing, shout, or say amen. I want to make a distinction, however, between joyful noise and offensive noise in worship by looking at the concept of noise as it is seen in the prophet Amos and in Psalm 100.

First, the words of the prophet Amos are clear. They are terse and bold. He says, "Take away from me the noise of your songs, I will not listen to the melody of your harps" (Amos 5:23). God is offended by the semblance of worship that is not grounded in the substance of God's character. Worship has to reflect the fact that God is a God of justice and righteousness. If we are to worship God in spirit and truth, then we need to be true to ourselves and to the essence of the message of God as revealed to the prophets.

Worship is more than harmonized or syncopated noise. In this context "noise" is anything that does not aid in bringing about a change in the condition of life for those who are victims of injustice and unrighteousness. Noise is celebration without commitment to liberation. Noise can be loud or soft; conceivably, it can be silence. It can be sophisticated or simplistic.

In terms of church music, noise may be anthems sung in the European tradition or some contemporary gospel music. Noise is singing and saying that which is not reflected in our practice of agape. Paul, in writing to the Corinthians, explains offensive noise by stating: "If I speak in the tongues of mortals and of angels, but do not have love, I am a noisy gong or a clanging cymbal" (1 Cor. 13:1).

When there is authentic worship in church, it is also felt in society. More precisely, the worship experience that occurs in churches throughout the United States is not an isolated phenomenon. The church cannot claim genuinely to worship God if that worship reflects no evidence of concern for the oppressed throughout the world. If this is the case, then the church is indeed filled with noise. Clearly noise is not related to volume, intensity, tone, or pitch. For example, a song may be performed perfectly, but those who sing must strive to live the message of the song. This likewise applies to those who preach, teach, pray, and counsel.

The idiom "actions speak louder than words" is true for both the preacher and the parishioner. Dick Gregory, speaking in a Virginia church, assailed blacks for their silence and inaction on the slavery of blacks in South Africa. He effectively said that blacks in America were unique in their silence toward the artrocious dehumanization of their South African black brothers and sisters. Apartheid in South Africa and poverty in other Third World countries are removed from the conscience of black Americans. This is precisely why the focus of worship must not be so eschatological that it fails to consider the prevailing conditions of poor and oppressed people. The church is a microcosm of the black community and its constituents are a reflection of society. This means that the church has resident poor and oppressed to help and heal. Those in the black church have been heavily influenced by the white evangelical model, which tends to separate religion from life and faith from action and is more prone to participate in misunderstanding the nature of God with regard to justice and righteousness for all people at all times. In other words, what we do in church is not isolated from what we do outside of the worship experience.

This brings us to the concept of joyful noise in worship. While offensive noise is expression that does not reflect a consciousness that is cognizant of a God who liberates the oppressed, joyful noise is the exact opposite. Joyful noise takes place when we become conscious of liberation as a constitutive element in the nature of God. While I understand that it is sometimes difficult to discern the joyful from the offensive because of our different levels of understanding and involvement, I believe that when one becomes fully conscious of the power and grace of God, we are compelled to make a joyful noise. When God becomes a present reality in our worship there is a spontaneous gushing forth of joy. O what a noise! What a joyful noise! As our faith develops and grows and our consciousness of God heightens, our joy also increases. The psalmist plainly tells us:

> Make a joyful noise to the LORD, all the earth.
> Worship the LORD with gladness;
> Come into his presence with singing.
> Know that the LORD is God.
>
> (Psalm 100:1-3a)

When worship is totally devoted to God, grounded in love and humility, and devoid of any semblance of egoism, we then experience the "unspeakable joy" that has characterized the black church from its brush arbor days to the present.

Integrative Worship

Worship in the black church should be integrative and holistic. The entire worship service should be biblically and morally oriented in order to allow God's Word to speak to the condition of the individual and society. A church that believes in God's power to change the world believes in justice and equality for all. This is reflected in the sermon, music, and stewardship practices of the parishioners. All elements of worship fit together and help to harmonize the individual and community.

In order for the black church to affect lives beyond the walls of the sanctuary and far beyond Sunday morning, the preacher and people will have to come together and resolutely affirm that God is not only a God of love, whose son Jesus saves from sin, but that God is a God of justice and righteousness. Consequently, Jesus not only redeems us, but also frees us from whatever is oppressive and dehumanizing. Our task is to integrate the power and spirit evident on Sunday morning into the everyday life of the church and community. Essentially, I am suggesting that the church and its mission are not isolated entities but correlates to the world and its social problems. Too often blacks have been influenced by conservative evangelicals and televangelists who seldom, if ever, deal with questions of distributive justice, social and political power, or freedom from oppression.

The task of worship in the black church is to be true to our heritage and to God. When I look around urban and rural areas, I see people hurting and in trouble. This suggests that preachers and laypersons have an awesome responsibility in trying to do the will of God. We have to construct public worship in a way that will help change society to what we believe God would have it to be. This means that Sunday morning activities are intricately connected to the daily lives of people. Worship, liberation, and social change go hand in hand.

Black Music in Worship

Music in the black church needs to reflect the struggles and hopes of blacks and not be an imitation of white European music. Blacks should be skeptical and cautious about incorporating the resources of the oppressor in the worship experience of the oppressed. Music is an expression that grows out of the joys, suffering, and pains of black people as they experience life in the midst of socioeconomic injustices. If it does not speak to particular concerns and does not grow out of the African tradition, it will fail to alter the oppressive course of events that we face daily. Wyatt Tee Walker, in his book *Somebody's Calling My Name: Black Sacred Music and Social Change*, points out that the black church that does not sing "the songs of Zion"—spirituals and gospels—is divorcing itself from its cultural heritage and is in effect joining the culture of the oppressor. Walker states: "It is patently clear that people at worship should be singing the music that relates directly to their social context. The social context of black people is the need for liberation from racism and oppression."[4] The black church realizes that this is an uncontroverted fact. Despite the privileged status of some, it must be able to change the structure of its worship to recapture its heritage—where the music is pregnant with emotion and understanding that are directly related to the social and political reality of black people. Walker, an eminent pastor and leader in the struggle for social change, directly relates liberation and social change to the worship components of the black church.

> If black people are to pursue the most direct route to liberation via religion, there is a need for them to embrace the music which in large measure has demonstrated its relevance and usefulness in resisting racism and oppression. The black church, then, as the chief reservoir of Black Sacred Music, holds a vast potential for a ministry of *social change* at both the personal and collective levels. Collective liberation can only follow personal liberation.[5]

The mass-oriented black church contrary to the class-oriented retain more of their African roots and have been responsible for fueling the liberation struggle. "It has been the churches peopled with the masses which have retained the music and worship style that is identifiably Africa linked and which have been in the forefront of much of the struggle for liberation."[6]

Gospel music and spirituals tend to reflect the social conditions of society and represent the depth of sorrow and suffering experienced by blacks in the context of their everyday life. Although gospel music followed spirituals and lined-out hymns in the music tradition of the independent black churches, and though it once was more prevalent in the Pentecostal-Holiness churches, it is now a part of the mainline black church. Portia K. Maultsby makes this clear:

> Because gospel music expressed the essence of contemporary black culture, it has moved beyond the boundaries of the Holiness-Pentecostal churches into many mainline black churches, ranging from Baptist to Catholic parishes. Mellonee Burnim sums up the importance of gospel in present day black religion by stating, "in the same way that the negro spiritual was fundamental to the religion of the black slave, so is gospel music the backbone of contemporary black religion."[7]

Worship in the black church is enhanced by music that the churchgoers love and enjoy. The most meaningful worship experience uses a variety of musical idioms, and gospel music and spirituals seem to speak to the needs of black people. Blacks have systematically been placed on the bottom side of the American socioeconomic and political agenda. This is where poverty and injustice are visibly evident. Moreover, the struggle to maintain one's sanity and sense of dignity is exacerbated by a system that blames the victim rather than those who perpetrate injustice. Therefore, when blacks come to church to worship, they do not want to hear a sterile and emotionless rendition of an anthem written by and for the oppressors. They are not interested in music that they cannot relate to, and simply does not help them cope with the reality of oppression. The majority of people want to hear from the Lord and want God to speak through the lyrics, cadences, and tunes that make their "burdens lighter, and brighten up their day."

The gospel song "We Need to Hear from You" by Sandra Crouch has meaning to most blacks because it speaks to the needs of blacks who see God as the ultimate and decisive mediator between themselves and the oppressor:

> We need to hear from You
> Lord, we need a word from You
> If we don't hear from You, Lord,
> What will we do? Oh, my Lord,
> We're wanting you more and more each day,
> To show us your perfect way
> There is no other way that we can live.[8]

Hearing from the Lord enables African Americans to deal with their life situation in a way that brings personal peace and satisfaction as well as a change in the condition of their existence. It expresses our vulnerability by implying that there are many voices to be heard, but there is only one voice that we need. Without that voice, we are hopelessly lost; conversely, with that voice from God, we can live! We can cope! We can make it!

Moreover, singing a song like the black spiritual "Joshua Fit De Battle Ob Jerico" shows that the fighting spirit still resides in the souls of blacks and in their worship.

> Joshua fit de battle ob Jerico and de
> Walls came tumbling down
> Up to de walls of Jerico
> He marched with spear in han'
> "Go blow dem horns," Joshua cried
> "Kase de battle am in my han."
> Joshua commanded de chillen to shout
> An' de wall came tumblin' down.
> Wasn't that a mighty day O Lord,
> When Joshua fit de battle of Jerico.[9]

This spiritual expresses the hope that like Joshua, black people can with the help of God fight and win against the odds.

The music in the black church undoubtedly speaks to the troubles, pains, fears, joys, and sorrows of those who come to church truly to worship. The music generally sets the tone of the worship experience, and gospel music is connected to the life experience of most African Americans who have not forgotten their slave heritage and their current troubles. For those who are proud of their culture, this music speaks, as no other, to the history, hopes, and dreams of black people who are still "coming up on the rough side of the mountain."

Preaching for Liberation

The sermon is the heart of the worship experience. Most have heard it said that "if the minister can't preach, he is doomed in the black church." Although there is a growing perception of preaching today as tantamount to "whooping, squawling, and hollering," the black minister must be a responsible heralder of the gospel. This responsibility means merging good, authentic homiletic form and substance into a powerful sermon. It is simply not enough for preachers or parishioners to shout and sing. While emotion is very important and preaching style critical to the overall message, the black preacher has a moral and theological responsibility to develop a sound hermeneutical approach to the gospel. The preacher is compelled to say something that addresses the needs of the people, directing the message to their heart and head. This wholistic message will teach blacks how to live as Christians and how to relate their religion to freedom practices.

Those who support the church and its ministry need to hear a word of power and spirit—a word of liberation. This preaching "in demonstration of the spirit and of power"[10] must speak to the total condition of the black community.

The sermon needs to be powerful enough to motivate churchgoers to live a life that reflects the spirit of Jesus Christ. The preacher has to be able to assuage the fears and strengthen the hopes that reside in the bosom of our people. After a soul-stirring sermon, few can sing "My hope is built on nothing less than Jesus' blood and righteousness"[11] with the verve and enthusiasm displayed in the black church. This enthusiasm is a manifestation of faith in a God who is able "to carry you [us] through." With the help of the preacher, blacks are able to celebrate in spite of the reality of oppression and injustice because they believe that God is faithful and just. Henry Mitchell captured the essence of this assertion: "The best gospel preaching is at once proclamation and celebration. . . . A part of the genius of black preaching has been its capacity to generate this very kind of celebration, despite the hardest circumstances. . . . Preaching without celebration is de facto denial of the good news, in any culture."[12] The preacher celebrates and encourages others to celebrate; however, the preaching ministry must also include liberation. Without liberation, there can be no authentic celebration.

The preacher leads blacks to understand that their celebration and spiritual experience are the flip side of a depressed social experience. Though black people can celebrate in good and bad times, the preacher has the responsibility of helping transform the bad times into good times where the oppressed will have jobs, adequate housing, and the ability to determine their own destiny. With the help of God, this can be accomplished during our lifetime.

6

Christian Education

I am giving you these instructions, Timothy, my child, in accordance with the prophecies made earlier about you, so that by following them you may fight the good fight, having faith and a good conscience. By rejecting conscience, certain persons have suffered shipwreck in the faith, among them are Hymenaeus and Alexander, whom I have turned over to Satan, so that they may learn not to blaspheme.

—1 Timothy 1:18-20

The passage from 1 Timothy no doubt springs to the mind of any deacon in the black church who, week after week, testifies that the Lord has been good and that a "shipwreck" will not be made of his or her life. During these prayer meetings, which are as much a part of black church life as morning worship, the preacher learns of the aches and pains, sorrows, burdens, fears, disappointments, and struggles of those who constitute the black church. Here black people express special and unique experiences that need to be understood and incorporated into the practice of Christian education. Christian education, therefore, needs to understand the context of black life and appreciate the parallels between black cultural history and the biblical message.

However, the black church in particular, like the Christian church in general, is something less than it should be and more often than not much less than the Lord requires, being too often a victim of structuralism and the vain babblings of its members. We have confused religiosity with spirituality, church membership with salvation, and positions with persons—indeed, works with faith.

Understanding the Context

Neither Christian education nor education in general is a priority for the majority in the church. We are a preaching-oriented people, who display a marked lack of support for serious Bible study, workshops, seminars, and general training in spiritual and liberation development. In addition, we have failed to apply the teachings of Jesus to particular needs that exist among blacks. Many who flock to church systematically and participate in a potpourri of activities and auxiliaries have failed to live out the connection between what is done in church and how we approach and respond to our families, communities, neighbors, and colleagues.

For too many, the church is no longer a place where love radiates from "heart to heart and breast to breast." It has become a victim of our new, more sophisticated psychology—we simply mask our hate, sublimate our anger, and pretend to understand. Instead of coming to church to learn more about Jesus, freedom, and justice, we fake our knowledge and vehemently defend our ignorance. Instead of growing spiritually and educationally, we attend church to frown upon the faithful and nurture the doubt that resides in our minds by luring others into sharing our disbelief. This heresy in the church must be replaced with a liberating educational ministry based on the teachings of Jesus and his disciples. Otherwise, we shall indeed end up with a "shipwrecked faith" such as Hymenaeus and Alexander. We need a new understanding of Paul's message when he writes, "I am giving you these instructions, Timothy, my child, in accordance with the prophecies made earlier about you, so that by following them you may fight the good fight" (1 Tim. 1:18).

Christian life is a battle against wickedness in high places and sometimes in the church. It certainly can be likened unto a battle, especially for the minister who is trying to bring about liberation and social change through the church's teaching ministry. The Scripture says, "So that by following them you may fight the good fight." The black Christian's life, and especially the minister's life, is indeed a *good fight*. The layperson and the preacher are in a war. We are fighting a battle. There are some battles in the church and world worth waging. A good fight is a fight against oppression, evil, and apathy. A good fight is against unfairness, injustice, poverty, racism, sexism, militarism, and domination. It is against the forces of ignorance. That is why Paul says, Timothy, you have to fight a good fight because there is evil and ignorance not only in the world, but in the church. You must fight the power of Satan! Timothy, this is no time to be tepid and torpid. You cannot be afraid, nor can you be lukewarm; you cannot be indifferent because this good fight is for the glory of God. This is the substance of Christian life. It means standing up to that which is evil, wrong, and false. Moreover, Paul reminds Timothy that God had chosen him for this ministry. He had been called to do the work of Christ; therefore, he should fight on and not fall victim to those who did not know better or those who did not respect him.

Education as a Weapon

Christian education is one of the church's most enduring weapons against evil, ignorance, and injustice. The church is compelled to spread the gospel by teaching blacks how to love and respect themselves and others, how to succeed and excel, and how to fight the forces of oppression. Christian education in the black church, however, is often lacking in structure and overall systematic goals. Because the church has traditionally been considered a worshiping institution, it has often failed to develop proper facilities for educational ministry. This has contributed to the difficulty that Christian education has faced in becoming a part of the structure of the black church experience. Certainly, most churches today have a structured Sunday church school; however, Christian education is more than that, and this is where black theology comes in. Its point of entry in the black church is through the educative process. In becoming a part of the practice of ministry it can focus and direct black religion toward liberation. Dr. J. Deotis Roberts says, "The involvement of black theology in the educative process should begin with Christian education in the local churches and should move through the denominational and ecumenical agencies of our churches. It should reach not only children and youth, it should reach adults."[1]

The battle for Christian education is a battle to fight evil, disinterest, ignorance, and heresy in church and society. This fight is unlike others because the weapons are different—the primary weapons are faith and a good conscience. "I am giving you these instructions . . . that you may fight the good fight, having faith and a good conscience." Faith and a good conscience are interconnected. Blacks seem to have always known that faith is one way we can stand against the forces of evil. The "shield of faith" has protected us when we have been assailed by doubt and trouble. Faith is critical to the life of the church because the fight against injustice and evil cannot be won without the strength that comes from faith and a good conscience.

Christian education strengthens our faith and equips us with the tools to fight injustice and indifference. Black theology helps us understand that "God don't like ugly," and God is on the side of those who have been mistreated and oppressed. It is a major tool to be used in the battle against the evil that is so much a part of the social and political system. However, it is also a critical and necessary ingredient in the battle toward self-understanding, self-criticism, and the development of an education program that will help to usher in the day of freedom for the black laity and those of us who practice ministry.

First Things First

Christian education in the church is the process and content of teaching about the life of Jesus Christ and applying these concepts to every phase of the church's ministry. Christian education, then, permeates the church's entire ministry with the liberation message of Jesus Christ. It takes place not simply during Sunday school, but in meetings of choirs, ushers, auxiliaries, boards, and committees—whenever the church worships, prays, make plans, or works.

The educational ministry of the church must understand its task in broad terms. This means that before we start discussing theology in any form, we need to meet people where they are. Some will first need to be taught to read and write. Yes, there are persons within the black church who cannot do either. Many of these children and adults are afraid to let others know of their limitations. The church could begin with a literacy program designed to help people master the basics so they can begin to function at a level of competence.

In addition, a tutorial program is needed in every black church in America. It is a tragedy that so many young people are dropping out of high school or receiving failing grades while the church sits by idly. Most churches have professionals within their ranks who are quite capable and willing to assist in the education of our young people. One or two nights a week should be set aside for tutoring and studying in order to help children and adults master the basics. For example, in our church there is a Homework Assistance Program designed to serve this function.

The black church historically has been an educational institution—providing facilities and resources to help start our colleges and institutes. In today's society, our children, youth, and adults need all the help they can get. Christian education must involve the church and family in the total life of black people. Shirley Chisholm, writing in a monograph edited by Joseph Washington, says:

> At each and every black church in the United States, there should be an education unit dedicated to the development and implementation of strategies to improve the education of our children. . . . Most importantly, the church is that segment of the black community where we can most successfully address the question of our economic resources and how they can be channelled to the benefit of black education.[2]

Christian education in the church is responsible for bridging the gap between the teachings of the Bible and socioeconomic reality in the black community.

Christian Education in Context

In the black church, Christian education has to be about freedom and liberation. Consequently, teaching people to read and study, to respect themselves and others, and to practice love and peace in the context of the black community will lead to what Paulo Freire calls "education for critical consciousness."[3] Black theology is the paradigm for teaching black Christians how to practice the teachings of Jesus and the prophets. In fact, the black church should be the key actor in bringing about liberation, transformation, and social change.

Monumental Baptist Church

Although the church has been passive in effectuating change, some ministers have been actively pursuing efforts that will eventually alter the condition of life for many blacks. For example, in Pittsburgh, Pennsylvania, Monumental Baptist Church, under the able leadership of the Reverend T. E. Smith, is trying to bring about liberation and change. They are developing a Home Mission Institute that will be designed to address the issues of inadequate housing, joblessness, illiteracy, and poverty. In addition, the pastor has led the church to develop a pool of volunteers to serve on committees and boards in the community. Smith serves as moderator of a coalition that seeks to ensure equal employment opportunity for blacks. This organization reviews the affirmative action plans of federal, state, local, and corporate agencies. As part of the Home Mission Institute, the church plans to house a literacy program.

Moreover, the ministry at Monumental Baptist Church has focused on bringing pastors and churches in Pittsburgh together in order to develop the political power to address the sociopolitical and economic conditions of blacks in that city. The pastor is gradually but systematically trying to get the laity to see the importance of accepting responsibility for their quality of life based on the political decisions that are made for and by the community.

Reverend Smith has launched an optimistic and thoroughgoing Christian education program for effectuating social change. However, he has been hampered by the relatively small black population in the area and the corresponding lack of black leadership. He argues that many of the leaders who are in place see themselves as "defenders of the status quo."[4]

Canaan Baptist Church of Christ

Another black American church that is changing the social and political life of its people and community is Canaan Baptist Church of Christ in Harlem, where Dr. Wyatt Tee Walker is pastor. Walker is known for his active role in the Civil Rights movement during the Martin Luther King, Jr. era and beyond, and for his contributions to the betterment of American society through his writings and preaching. A minister of international renown, Walker has led his congregation in the development of several programs that have impacted positively upon the community. Canaan Baptist Church has developed a Senior Citizens Service Center that has grown from a one-day-a-week program serving twenty persons in 1972 to a full-scale service center serving the senior citizens of central Harlem. Dr. Walker says,

> By 1981, 1600 registered seniors were served by our center. Our staff had grown to 31 full-time and part-time workers. Our corps of volunteers consist of approximately 27 persons. Over 300 seniors per month are served by the combined programs of the center. The center has not limited its role to being a service provider. We are also advocates for the rights of seniors and for improvement of their conditions. The center's staff members have assumed significant roles in community action and legislative changes on a local and national level. . . . We have led petition drives and rallies against the Reagan administration's budget cuts which would be devastating to the elderly and poor.[5]

In addition to this comprehensive program designed to meet the needs of the elderly and poor in Harlem, Walker also led the church in developing a federal credit union and many other programs that will help his congregation become liberated.

Other Churches

Several other churches have specific programs to educate our children and adults in ways that will lead to freedom and liberation. At Concord Baptist Church of Christ in Brooklyn, Dr. Gardner C. Taylor urges other black churches to emulate his former congregation by establishing funds to aid young people's community groups. In Washington, D. C., Shiloh Baptist Church, under the leadership of Dr. Henry C. Gregory, now deceased, developed a black youth project to help minister to young people in the depressed areas of the city.

Throughout the country, black churches are working to help change the conditions of life for our people. "Project SPIRIT, a pilot program of after-school tutorials at 15 churches in Oakland, Indianapolis, and Atlanta, has substantially improved the reading, writing and arithmetic skills of six- to twelve-year-olds and made them more aware and proud of their cultural heritage."[6] In Oakland, California, Dr. J. Alfred Smith, Sr. has developed an excellent model for education and community transformation. Several studies have been done on Pastor Smith and the ministries at Allen Temple. Several other pastors, such as Dr. H. Beecher Hicks, Jr., Dr. Charles Booth, Rev. Roscoe Cooper, Rev. Kevin Cosby, Rev. Buster Soaries, Dr. Frank Reid, Jr., Dr. James Perkins, Rev. E. K. Bailey, and others have developed programs to help transform the black community by addressing the specific needs of black youths and the black male. At Second Baptist Church in Richmond, Virginia, several new community outreach ministries are beginning that are aimed to address the issues facing the black male and all of us who must deal with the complexities of the urban milieu.

The black church exists in a historical, social, political, and economic context, not in our imagination or in some abstract theory. This means that what the church does is not isolated in time and space. In the same connection, the prophets, Moses, Jesus Christ, and Paul of Tarsus operated out of a particular context—geographical, social, political, and historical. The basically urban context of the black church today means that its message must reflect the reality of this troubled situation. Poverty, homelessness, joblessness, drug addiction, crime, and myriad other afflictions have gripped the black community. In this situation the black church must function as a teacher of the gospel message. In this context black theology comes face to face with sociopolitical reality.

Conformity versus Liberation

Public education is designed to establish conformity and homogeneity. Black students are expected to learn more about Western civilization than about Africa or the history of slavery in the United States. Furthermore, the irony is that achievement in school is measured by how much one actually knows about the oppressor.

The lack of meaningful multicultural curriculum in public education is extremely debilitating to blacks. The fact that there is a decreasing number of black teachers in public education while the number of black students is increasing exacerbates the cultural and racial schism in schools. To further compound the problem, the resegregation of public schools (for example, in Norfolk, Virginia) has isolated and alienated the poor under the supposedly benign and innocent guise of neighborhood schools.[7] "Neighborhood schools" is generally understood as a code word for segregation or resegregation. One does not have to be an urban geographer to know that most neighborhoods are racially identifiable, that is, segregated.

It is important to know what some educational theorists have said in order for pastors, lay persons, and Christian education planners to think comprehensively about education and understand that Christian education in the black church is a mammoth task. Nevertheless, the mission of the church is to develop ways to teach young blacks how to excel in our highly skilled and technological society.

Student achievement is a very important subject of research and debate. The factors contributing to achievement vary from the cleanliness of the building and the size of the school and class to family background and IQ. Christopher Jencks, James Coleman, Arthur Jensen, and Michael Rutter are four well-known theorists who have contributed in one way or another to our understanding of public education and student achievement.[8] Also, John Dewey and Lawrence A. Cremin have impacted significantly the development of educational theory and practice.[9] While these philosophers and educators have developed interesting theoretical formulations about the issues in education, none has been as illuminating regarding the plight of black children in the educational arena as the theoretical formulations of African social anthropologist John U. Ogbu. Ogbu's concept of *caste minorities* strikes at the heart of the problem that blacks experience in the American educational arena. He distinguishes between three types of minorities: autonomous minorities, caste minorities and immigrant minorities.[10] Blacks in the United States are a caste minority. In describing this group, Ogbu states:

> The dominant group usually regards them as inherently inferior in all respects. . . . Their economic, ritual, and political roles are often sharply defined. The kinds of work they do are usually [the necessary but dirty, demeaning, and unpleasant jobs for their superiors]. In general caste minorities are not allowed to compete for the most desirable roles on the basis of their individual training and abilities. The least desirable roles they are forced to play are generally used to demonstrate that they are naturally suited for their low position in society. Thus their political subordination is reinforced by their economic subordination.[11]

Ogbu suggests that the American caste system is basically responsible for the failure of blacks in the educational system. Therefore, most of the efforts to reform public education have failed to address the fact that failure is perpetuated by the structure and goals of the system. This means that compensatory educational programs, integration, equal educational opportunity, access to education, and other reforms have done little to boost black achievement and bridge the gap between blacks and whites. Blacks receive an inferior education even within a system that looks fair and equitable. He states that

> Blacks who attend the same schools as whites presumably share equal facilities, funding, and staffing with the latter, but they still do not perform as well. The reason for lower black performance lies partly in the way that schools and their classrooms operate, which involves subtle devices to differentiate black training from white in such a way that the former is inferior whether or not it is given in the same schools and classrooms.[12]

Ogbu argues that schools encourage the failure of blacks in subtle ways that range from low expectations by the teachers to disproportionately placing black children in classes for those with mental disabilities. He states that

> the schools unconsciously encourage black students to fail academically, to drop out of school earlier than white students, and to enter postschool society with just so much education as the dominant group considers appropriate for their traditional social and technoeconomic roles. By repeating this process generation after generation, the schools help to maintain and rationalize the job ceiling and other caste barriers against blacks.[13]

Since blacks are more likely to be unemployed and therefore economically unsuccessful or poor, the black church has to do what the schools and some parents cannot do. It has to boost achievement by teaching self-esteem and self-reliance. Positive self-esteem is a prerequisite for achievement in school and society.

The church also must develop programs to enable black children and adults to become culturally literate, teaching the importance of Harriet Tubman, Sojourner Truth, W. E. B. Dubois, Carter G. Woodson, Nat Turner, Malcolm X, Martin Luther King, Jr., and the nameless others who have labored for freedom and justice. We need to learn our own history and the value of our contributions to the development of society and the quest for freedom. This means that Sunday school and other church activities need to combine teaching the Bible with black history and current social concerns. This Afrocentric focus needs to permeate the educational activities and can be accomplished through the participation of the church, parents, and community in creating an environment conducive to the effective education of black children.

The black church can use the information of the educational theorists by expecting more from everyone involved in the education process and emphasizing the importance of biblical education in the liberation of blacks. The church must begin to read, debate, study, and discuss ways of achieving freedom and enhancing self-esteem. Inasmuch as schools are not interested in teaching blacks the skills to liberate themselves, the church is compelled to do so, and the preacher will have to lead the way by sometimes teaching church school, leading seminars, conducting workshops, and training children, youth, adults, and anyone who is willing to help in the work of the ministry. Without the active involvement of the pastor, liberation education is not likely to occur in the black church.

While blacks have failed to succeed in public education because of the reasons cited earlier, Christian education helps to assure success by teaching moral values and self-respect. Moreover, Christian education in the black church has to counter the subtle messages of inferiority that are systematically conveyed through the public education process. Black theology, when incorporated in the Christian education process, helps teachers, church leaders, children, and young adults to understand the need for liberation and the methods by which it can be achieved. The motto of the United Negro College Fund, "The mind is a terrible thing to waste," also describes the objective of black theology in the education process. We must begin to think critically and to assess honestly our commitment to education for liberation and take responsibility for eradicating the oppression, poverty, and injustice that grip our community.

The black church needs to teach liberation with the same commitment that public schools have in teaching algebra and English literature. If we begin to teach children in the church the importance of their history and culture, and the truth about racism, injustice, and poverty, then we will begin to compete with the enemies who are simply teaching conformity in the schools. The black church has to provide an alternative to the philosophy of conformity, and that alternative is a theology and education that liberates.

This can be done through the development of daycare facilities and church-operated schools that address the needs of our urban children and youth. For example, at the church where I serve as pastor, we are in the process of establishing an educational program with an Afrocentric focus that will house pre-school and early childhood children. This Center for Urban Education and Child Development will also use the theories of John Ogbu and others in order that the minority caste status of blacks will not hamper their aspirations and hopes as they plan and prepare for the future.

The black church has the resources and the commitment to alter the negative effects of public education on the achievement and aspirations of blacks. We need to realize the urgency of our task and begin to intervene at the earliest possible level in order that black children will no longer have to depend on the architects of discrimination and injustice to teach them how to succeed in the struggle for freedom and liberation.

Effective Sunday Schools

Education in the church is multidimensional; however, Sunday school is one critical area in which education ministry can be enhanced. While Sunday schools are declining in most black churches, there are some churches that have very successful programs.

Sid Smith chronicles the growth of ten black Sunday schools in his book *10 Super Sunday Schools in the Black Community*.[14] In each of these thriving

Sunday schools, the pastor plays a leading role in their growth and development. The active involvement of the pastors in the promotion, teaching, training, and program development process contributes to their effectiveness. In addition, Smith emphasizes the importance of well-trained teachers who are committed to the gospel in addition to the special needs of adults. However, I am disturbed by his assertion that a theologically conservative approach to the Bible contributes to success. Most of the churches that Smith describes are affiliated with the Southern Baptist Convention and use their literature and materials. While I believe that most Southern Baptists are relatively uninterested in the liberation of blacks and poor, I think that learning styles and methods of teaching can be studied and adapted to the more radical needs of the black church.

Two of the ministers whom Smith upholds as examples of leadership have been prominently associated with Jerry Falwell, who is clearly out of touch with the goals and aspirations of progressive and conscientious blacks. Dr. E. V. Hill, Pastor of Mount Zion Missionary Baptist Church in Los Angeles, and Dr. J. Herbert Hinkle, pastor of the Cathedral of Faith in Inkster, Michigan have apparently balanced their association with prominent archconservatives with other social ministries that meet the needs of people in their communities.[15] Having heard the inspiring sermons of E. V. Hill at the late-night services of the National Baptist Convention's Congress on Christian Education, I know that his ability to "tell the story" accounts in large measure for his popularity among conservatives and liberals, black and white. He is simply one of the most eloquent preachers of our time!

The black Sunday school cannot afford to be a carbon copy of the white evangelical Sunday school. Mary Love convincingly argues that there is an absence of good black images in Sunday school curriculum:

> Many black Sunday Schools use curriculum developed by nondenominational agencies or publishers who follow the mode of modern marketing techniques viewed to achieve profit and satisfy the major market. Repeatedly, these publishers will be tokenistic and give some semblance of concern for the black market by strategically placing and timing one or two black images. However, few, if any, blacks are involved in the development of this curriculum. What type of image does this convey to the black child? As a result, the image being planted is that of the majority, which leads to the development of an inferiority complex.[16]

Black Sunday schools need to place liberation education and spiritual growth above all other objectives. Yes, numerical growth is important, but our freedom and self-esteem are essential to our ontology and existence. If the church has to sacrifice liberation in order to grow numerically, then it might as well be dead—no, it is dead! The goal of church growth and Sunday school growth in the black community is to foster social change by helping blacks understand that the message of the Bible, indeed the message of Jesus, is one of freedom and liberation. Without this general and comprehensive understanding there can be no real growth, no matter how large the numbers are.

Effective Christian education in the black church demands a careful analysis of curriculum materials to detect any semblance of racism and obviate it by supplementary materials or a completely different, nontraditional curriculum. The serious and committed pastor and church may have to write their own material or simply teach from the Bible until the needs of blacks are addressed by publishers who write literature for church schools. For example, at Second Baptist Church we are exploring these and other options as we seek to focus on the importance of church school in the development of faith and self-esteem.

The Content of Christian Education

The task of Christian education in the church is to prepare people for liberation by understanding the Bible. This may require a new understanding of Sunday school, auxiliaries, and all areas of the teaching ministry of the church. What I am saying is that the black church does a disservice to blacks by emulating the white church. However, the first order of business for the church is to deprogram the clergy and laity who are victims of miseducation and self-hatred manifested in their tendency to regard too highly the ideas and practices of whites. Too many fail to appreciate their own culture, history, and tradition. A number of blacks are still reading the Bible and teaching through the eyes of whites, failing to capture and transmit to others the sense of liberation and hope that runs throughout the Bible.

In this connection, *The Kairos Document* is not only a prophetic challenge to the church in South Africa, but it is a challenge to the church everywhere—especially the black church in the United States. Black preachers and laypersons should heed the urgency of its words concerning sin and oppression:

> The Bible, of course, does not only describe oppression, tyranny and suffering. The message of the Bible is that oppression is sinful and wicked, an offense against God. The oppressors are godless sinners and the oppressed are suffering because of the sins of their oppressors. But there is hope because Yahweh, the God of the Bible, will liberate the oppressed from their suffering

and misery. He will redeem their lives from exploitation and outrage (Ps. 74:14). "I have seen the miserable state of my people in Egypt. I have heard their appeal to be free of their slave-drivers. I mean to deliver them out of the hands of the Egyptians." (Ex. 3:7)[17]

In the black church, Christian education focuses on understanding God through Jesus Christ as the liberator, redeemer, or deliverer. This theme of liberation must permeate the entire church curriculum. In *To You Who Teach in the Black Church*, James D. Tyms says:

> Until very recently, the main thrust in curriculum thinking and planning has been designed to perpetuate and lift to the highest levels of life the heritage of the white world, religiously and culturally. So effective was that design that black folk are still, for the most part, conditioned to think and feel that the white world lifts up the only significant curriculum content for the advancement of world culture and religious sainthood. . . . There has begun to emerge in the black world a consciousness that there are rich reservoirs of black heritage that can begin to be drawn upon to give rise to black pride, self-esteem and self-acceptance.[18]

The curriculum in the black church school needs to include a focus on liberation themes as found in the prophets and the words of Jesus as well as an understanding and appreciation of self. It appears that much of the Sunday school literature published by blacks, and almost all by whites, fails to address the specific and unique needs of the black church. We are still using the model that white evangelicals have developed. Simply stated, the black publishers, churches, congresses, and conventions need to be as devoted to liberation as the white conservative evangelicals are devoted to the issues that concern them.

Christian education and black theology, working in concert, can dramatically change our churches and communities. When we believe in our own abilities, hopes, and dreams, we can be free to cultivate those abilities and make our hopes and dreams a reality.

7

Self-esteem in the Black Church

I am somebody!

—*Jesse Jackson*

Love your neighbor as yourself.

—*Matthew 19:19*

The worth of persons has been at the forefront of ministry in the black church. The church has taught blacks that they are children of God long before the language of self-esteem became a part of their vocabulary. In the midst of slavery, Jim Crow laws, and overt racism, the black church was interpreting Scripture and experience to enhance the self-esteem of children and adults who were being dehumanized by laws and customs. This liberation motif inherent in the life and message of the church has sustained so many of us who are products of its teachings. When educational institutions, law-making bodies and businesses failed to accord full humanity to blacks, the black church was espousing a message of freedom and hope, challenging us to stand tall and be somebody in spite of the hostile and indifferent environment in which we lived.

Since the days of slavery in the antebellum South, blacks have always known that there was a contradiction between what whites said and what they did. They understood the words of Jesus, "Not everyone who says to me, 'Lord, Lord' will enter the kingdom of heaven" (Matt. 7:21).

The evangelical message of the African American church has been a message to enhance self-esteem and worth. The church historically has taught blacks that they had "worth" apart from socioeconomic status. We are not measured by what we have or do not have. A person's worth is not measured by economic possessions but by his or her understanding and commitment to God (cf. Matt. 6:33). Jesus says, "Therefore I tell you, do not worry about your life, what you will eat or what you will drink, or about your body, what you will wear. Is not life more than food,

115

and the body more than clothing? Look at the birds of the air; they neither sow nor reap nor gather into barns, and yet your heavenly Father feeds them! Are you not of more value than they?" (Matt. 6:25-26).

I remember growing up in the midst of poverty. We were a large family that had to struggle to make ends meet. Our house was a two-room "shanty" until my father and those of us who could assist began to add a few more rooms so we could move around. As late as 1964 we did not have electricity or running water. During my elementary school years, we used a kerosene lamp to study and read. I also know that we kept what we had clean and immaculate, and several of my brothers and sisters and I excelled in school. We had a hope that was deeply embedded in the bowels of our soul. We possessed what the apostle Paul calls "hope against hope" (cf. Rom. 4:18). This hope is the "stuff" that self-esteem is made of. It is the basic constitutive element inherent in the nature and structure of the self that knows God. The spirit of worth and self-esteem is seen in the nameless persons like me and numerous others who have been helped by the church's effort to stir up the hope that is in them.

Self-esteem is the crucial movement toward true evangelicalism, and the church's role is to raise the level of consciousness in our people so the message of the gospel may truly be liberative. The black church is called to actualize self-esteem in its ministry by developing programs that will specifically address this crucial need. There is a serious difference between what true evangelicalism is and what has been masquerading as evangelicalism. True evangelicalism is the liberating power of the gospel that enables persons to move toward positive self-esteem.

In order for blacks to change the condition of life in the urban centers of America, serious and drastic changes need to be made in their own lives. This introspection cannot be made by an outside agency or organization, but needs to come from within the individual nurtured by the Word of God as it is interpreted and practiced by the black church. Otherwise, change will not root in the heart and soul.

Black theology extrapolates those elements from the black experience that speak of strength, stamina, and hope in the face of suffering and degradation. It lifts up the positive while confronting the negative with honesty and integrity. The experience of any people is a mixture of good and bad, obedience and disobedience, and is best understood by that people. Black people in America have suffered much coming up through the years, and nobody can know or understand the trouble we have endured any better than we do. Nevertheless, neither romanticism nor self-pity is a way of overcoming this experience. Only by coming to grips with who we are, confronting the oppressive nature of society, and yearning to be free can we form the basis of a positive self-esteem that will manifest itself in individual and community transformation.

Self-esteem in Context

The African American has been subjected to the most persistent and blatant forms of racism and oppression to be inflicted upon a people during modern times. This has been done in the midst of a society that speaks of freedom and equality in lofty philosophical terms without any recognizable intent to comply with the moral obligation of its written or spoken words. Black people have done well to maintain their sanity in the midst of this constant and pervasive assault on their self-esteem.

Unfortunately, the systemic nature of injustice has had a serious effect on the self-esteem of many of our young people.[1] Poor self-esteem manifests itself in a lingering torpor that is both frightening and sad. In observing the behavior of some in the black community, I often see and hear about insecurity, insensitivity, anger, and violence directed against each other rather than against the "world rulers, principalities, and powers" (cf. Eph. 6:12) that are responsible for the oppression. There is a growing disregard for life and self-preservation evidenced by the increasing number of suicides, black-on-black crime, substance abuse, and so on. This implosive behavior is destroying the black community. Karl Menninger in *Man against Himself* states:

> Whoever studies the behavior of human beings cannot escape the conclusion that we must reckon with an enemy within the lines. It becomes increasingly evident that some of the destruction which curses the earth is self-destruction; the extraordinary propensity of the human being to join hands with external forces in an attack upon his own experience is one of the most remarkable of biological phenomena.[2]

Because the enemy is not so easily recognized, some blacks unknowingly have joined hands with the enemy and are gradually (and in many cases not so gradually) destroying themselves. Sigmund Freud's "death-instinct" seems to characterize the behavior of a growing percentage of our young people. In discussing the concept of "eros and thanatos," Menninger relates the example of doctors who are committed to saving or preserving life. In reference to the physician and patient he poignantly relates the following:

> Suddenly, or perhaps gradually, he becomes disillusioned. He discovers the patients often don't want to get well as much as they say they do. He discovers that their hovering and solicitous relatives often don't want them to get well either. He discovers that his efforts are combatted not alone by nature,

bacteria, and toxins, but by some imp of the perverse in the patient himself. . . . An old professor of mine once remarked that the physician must devote most of his efforts toward keeping the relatives from killing the patient, and then trust God—occasionally the surgeon—for the rest; but the skillful physician really does more. He not only holds off the relatives but he tries to keep the patient from doing those things which favor the disease rather than the recovery.[3]

In many ways, the black church and the preacher must be like the physician. They are compelled to become involved in an active effort to get the community "doing things which favor the recovery" of positive self-esteem and the desire to live and not foster self-destruction.[4]

The message of the church needs to focus upon enabling young people to understand that oppressive systems often create dysfunctional behavior among the oppressed. This new consciousness will help to put an end to self-destruction and direct our energies against the real enemy who often eludes us.

Taking Some Responsibility

While others may deserve the blame for the maladies that exist in the black community, we have to take control of the situation. Moreover, there is a need for a new method of ministering that will take into account the negative things that blacks do to themselves, such as black-on-black crime, teenage pregnancy, and community destruction. Though there are structural problems associated with these facts, the black community bears some of the burden for the problems and primary responsibility for the alleviation of these problems.

There is a correlation between self-image and many other aspects of one's life. Persons who think a lot of themselves seem to be markedly different from those who do not. There is a growing belief that blacks do not think highly of themselves and this self-derogation is a manifestation of a poor self-concept or low self-esteem. Conversely, blacks who are self-assured and possess a high level of self-esteem are often thought by others, especially whites, to be arrogant and aloof. Unfortunately, some blacks have embraced a negative view of themselves, a view that has been perpetuated and fueled by whites during and since the abolition of slavery. The systematic inculcation of demeaning and negative descriptions and characterizations of blacks has created a pathological problem in the black community manifested in negative behavior. The problem of low self-esteem or poor self-image seems to contribute to many of the maladies that exist in our communities.

When Jesse Jackson travels the width and breadth of this country leading black youth in the cheer "I am somebody," or "Up with hope and down with dope," he is not simply being poetic and oratorical. He is being prophetic—trying to alter the course of human events in order that the black community can be strengthened psychologically. This will lead to a greater level of achievement and productivity. Jackson, no doubt, is trying to instill a sense of worth and value in black youngsters in order that they will not become victims of self-annihilation or participants in the destruction of others.

If the poor, disenfranchised black child says "I am somebody" often enough, he or she may grow to believe it and act accordingly. This is a beginning step toward positive self-esteem. In the broad sense, self-esteem is possessing a positive image of one's capabilities and perception of worth. It means that one has a "good self-concept." "Self-concept is the sum total of the view which an individual has of himself. Self-concept is a unique set of perceptions, ideas and attitudes which an individual has of himself. The view which an individual has of himself is unique and to varying degrees is different from the view that anyone else has about him."[5]

The debate regarding the differences between self-concept and self-esteem, and the development of self-concept will be left to the psychologists and psychoanalysts. We are concerned about the possible manifestations of negative or poor self-esteem in the lives of black people. We have more of a gut feeling than scientific proof that the reality of negative actions is grounded in the psyche as a result of low self-esteem. The fact remains that the message of Jesse Jackson and other concerned leaders has become a part of the conscience or mind-set of a significant number of blacks, whether young or older adults. The transference of cultural stereotypes, however, is still prevalent in our society. Blacks have historically been described as lazy, shiftless, and no good. This description, coupled with the reality of socioeconomic deprivation, is often interpreted by our youths to mean that certain achievements are beyond the limits imposed upon them by society.[6]

Removing Impediments

In order to break down such stereotypes and accepted norms, the deification of some black cultural experiences is theologically inappropriate and practically suicidal because it unnecessarily highlights elements in the black experience that serve to impede the social progress of blacks. In this connection, the book by Henry Mitchell and Nicholas Cooper Lewter, *Soul*

Theology: The Heart of American Black Culture, is generally quite informative and adept in explicating the black experience. However, in discussing the majesty and omnipotence of God as it relates to soul theology they write:

> Outside the circles of organized black religion . . . the exclamation, "Good God A'mighty" may be heard almost anywhere, regardless of culture, both in church and on the street. The difference between the church and street is that the Lord's name is used with less inhibition on the streets. People swear by God Almighty, call on the same name in games of cards and craps, and generally manifest the visible amenities of respect for the deity out of all proportion to their obedience. They have inherited a cultural bias toward belief in God's inability to punish, and they want no part of blatant disrespect, no matter what their lack of commitment to the ways of Christ.[7]

Although this statement attempts to help us understand and respect God's power, it actually fails to do so because "swearing by God Almighty" and calling on God's name in crap games while manifesting "visible amenities of respect for deity out of proportion to obedience" is contradictory. These kinds of expressions may be cultural; however, they do not reflect any positive theological understanding nor do they characterize the essence of black cultural experiences. The example used by Mitchell and Lewter borders on the philosophical fallacy of equivocation because it assumes that using the Lord's name in any context has theological validity. Furthermore, the uninhibited use of the Lord's name is indicative of general disrespect for the deity and suggests a level of disobedience that is directly proportional to the disrespect evidenced by the careless language.

Biblical teachings admonish us not to call the Lord's name in vain (Deut. 5:11). God's name is holy, and to swear by God is to misunderstand the holiness of God and to possess a cheap understanding of God's omnipotence. This unholy posture should not be used to suggest or imply any thoroughgoing understanding of the power of God. Black youth need to understand that such talk and attitudes are unacceptable and culturally derogatory. A true understanding of God would foster self-respect, temperance, and positive self-esteem.

Blasphemous language must be seen for what it is; however, I agree that the spontaneity of it as well as the nonchalant attitude that accompanies such language is more a product of bad habits and negative environmental influences than anything else. The dehumanizing condition of black life manifested in joblessness, poor housing, substance abuse, poor health, and so on, contributes to a defeatist attitude among blacks who have been forced to exist on the bottom. The "been-down-so-long that down-don't bother-me" syndrome is really a facade for coping with the oppressive forces that so constantly inflict pain upon a people that their efforts to free themselves are systematically thwarted. John R. W. Stott says, "A low self-image is common, since many modern influences dehumanize human beings and make them feel worthless. Wherever people are politically or economically oppressed, they feel demeaned."[8]

Political and economic oppression is indeed demeaning. Blacks in America and other parts of the world such as South Africa have been victims of cruel and debased treatment for too long. It is really a miracle that blacks have been able to maintain their sanity in the midst of such hate and evil.

Understanding the Self

The self is a complicated phenomenon. Most people are constantly discovering and rediscovering elements about themselves that they did not know. This process of discovery is facilitated by the environment and other factors. Conversely, self-concept plays an active role in shaping one's experiences. David W. Felker says:

> The self-concept is a dynamic circular force in human lives. Every human is vitally influenced by those around him. The people who are important to him influence what he thinks of himself. The experiences which an individual has every day indicate to him that he is competent or incompetent, good or bad, worthy or unworthy. . . . The self-concept is forged by the pressures exerted upon an individual from the outside. But the self-concept also is an active ingredient in an individual's experiences. Experiences mold and shape the self-concept, but self-concept has an active dynamic role in shaping experiences.[9]

The circularity of self-concept also suggests that it is not a static phenomenon but is in the process of becoming. In a sense, Abraham Maslow's "self-actualization" or Carl Jung's "individuation" may be temporarily achieved depending upon the individual. However, one's self-concept can always be enhanced by experience and vice versa. How one thinks of oneself will determine, to some extent, the experiences one pursues or not for oneself and one's family. In this connection, the black minister's perceptions of the church and its role in society will affect the kind of activities, programs, and issues that he or she will develop and/or try to solve. The concerns that the minister identifies with are a reflection of his or her own self-perception. This basic idea has been held by several thinkers, including the noted philosopher William James. Indeed, the idea that self-perception is related to human behavior has been corroborated by several scholars who have found correlations between self-concept and achievement in school, contributions to society, as well as one's relationship to family and significant others.[10] Again, Jesse Jackson is correct in suggesting to young people that they think of themselves as important by emphasizing their value over and over again.

Self-esteem and Clergy

Black ministers must believe in their own ability to provide leadership for the church and the community. They must not succumb to the apathy that characterizes so many in the black community. As a public figure, counselor, preacher, and leader, the minister needs a high degree of self-esteem. Many look to him or her for guidance and direction. Moreover, men who are ministers are father figures for a significant number of black children who may be products of single-parent families. Such ministers must be self-assured, assertive, and decisive. They cannot afford to be timid, tepid, or weak in the church or community. The minister must face the forces of public policymakers that affect the life of black people with a new degree of assurance that asserts forthrightly that he or she is a proponent of justice and an ardent opponent of any individual or organization that seeks to oppress black people whether spiritually, politically, socially, or economically.

The black minister cannot forget that his or her basic source of support is the black community, specifically, the black church. As long as the minister is supported by these constituents and committed to the gospel of Jesus Christ, he or she is morally obligated to protect the oppressed from the disinterested wielders of power in city hall and other places. The minister who possesses high self-esteem will not acquiesce to the forces of self-interest and trade the freedom and self-determination of African Americans for his or her own desire for power and money. As long as some black ministers allow themselves to be "chosen" by whites as "leaders" in the black community in whatever capacity, there will be little or no substantive change in the social, political, and economic condition of our people. A new self-esteem is needed among the clergy—one that will enable ministers to be prophetic and strong, never succumbing to the lure of self-interest and self-satisfaction that has been used by whites to keep blacks virtually powerless.

The saying "I am somebody" or some other equivalent idiom can be used by pastors in black churches throughout America to help change the lives of our black children and youth. Maybe the pastor's self-perception as capable of impacting the lives of these young people needs to be enhanced. Certainly a nonchalant, resigned attitude will not help engender feelings of worthiness. Pastors must play an active role in the lives of young blacks in order to effectuate change in behavior and self-esteem.

Even if the pastor is actively involved in setting positive examples of what it means to think well of oneself, there is still a strong possibility that the impact of his or her involvement will be negligible; however, that should not deter him or her in the effort to help turn our young people around.

The role of the pastor in this process is critical and cannot be taken lightly. The development of positive self-esteem among black youth in the church is a major part of changing the direction of our youth. Since these are the future leaders and architects of justice in the church and society, the effort to help shape, guide, and direct young black church constituents is one of the minister's most important pastoral tasks. Developing effective self-esteem is much like developing effective schools. The late Ronald Edmonds, as well as other proponents of Effective Schooling,[11] have shown that the leader of the school must be involved in the total education process; likewise, the leader of the black church must be involved in changing the way young people think of themselves.

Dr. Martin Luther King, Jr. was involved in this way in the lives of those persons who fought and marched for freedom. What type of person was he? What enabled him to deal with a life of blatant oppression and abject mendacity in his quest for social, political, and economic reform? Black youth need to use King's life as a paradigm for understanding the self and developing positive self-esteem. But not just King! There are countless other persons within the local church who also qualify as mentors or models. Many of them are deacons, Sunday school teachers, or youth workers. They are unknown to the media and to those outside the confines of the local church. Yet they possess character and a positive self-image that radiates beyond their obscurity to challenge and encourage black children and youth in churches throughout the land.

Self-esteem and Black Youth

Young people are very concerned about how their peers see them, what their peers do, and how well they are accepted. "In other words, we might generalize that our feelings of self-worth and self-esteem grow in part from our perceptions of where we see ourselves standing in relation to persons whose skills, abilities, talents and aptitudes are similar to our own."[12] What I call "social homogeneity" seems to be the goal of a large number of young people. This is seen in the desire to wear designer jeans, unbuttoned shirts, similar haircuts, unfastened suspenders, and so on. The desire to be like everyone else is a strong trait in a group that is wrestling with the question of identity. Peer pressure is a formidable foe for young people and adults.

The most serious manifestation of a lack of positive self-esteem is seen, however, in the alarming numbers of sexually active and promiscuous teenagers. These young people do not seem to be concerned about the biblical concept of fornication. Indeed, many of them do not even know the meaning of the word, though they may have heard it in Sunday school. The problem of teenage pregnancy has reached epidemic status in the black community. Joyce A. Ladner, in an article published in *The State of Black America 1986*, states quite clearly that this is a very serious situation.

> There is no other problem in the black community today that is more threatening to future generations of families than teen pregnancy, a problem of monumental proportions that is producing the womanchild and manchild on unprecedented levels. It is a problem that will affect three generations—the teen parents, their children and the grandparents.[13]

This problem jeopardizes the stability of the black family and sets the black community back in its efforts to progress socially, economically, and educationally. It becomes increasingly difficult to finish school, get a job, and become self-supporting when there are children to raise. Consequently, many of these young people will have to seek government support and they will be trapped in the vicious cycle of poverty throughout their lives. "At any given time, sixty percent of children born to teenagers outside marriage, who lived and were not adopted, received welfare."[14]

Clearly, there is a negative intergenerational effect of teenage pregnancy that lingers on and on in such a way that many years afterward, few have been able to overcome the socioeconomic impact of raising a child while being a child. In the book *Risking the Future: Adolescent Sexuality, Pregnancy and Childbearing*, the authors state forthrightly some of the frightening consequences of teenage pregnancy.

> The conclusion one must draw from the existing research on the consequences of early childbearing is that women who become parents as teenagers are at greater risk of social and economic disadvantage throughout their lives than those who delay childbearing until their twenties. They are less likely to complete their education, to be employed, to earn high wages, and to be happily married; and they are more likely to have larger families and to receive welfare. . . . It is not only teenage mothers at risk. Their children are more vulnerable to a number of health risks, including disease, physical disability, and infant death. . . . Available evidence suggests that the children of teenage parents are especially prone to having children early in life themselves.[15]

The church must intervene in the personal lives of our young people by encouraging them to postpone sexual activity until marriage and adulthood.

How many of us have heard these teenagers explain that a baby gives them hope and something of their own, another human being to love and provide for. This is a sad phenomenon because the "reality principle" suggests that teenage pregnancy harbors difficulties that are long lasting. The love for the baby can soon turn to hate, resentment, and apathy when one has to abandon the promises of the future in order to fulfill the responsibility of raising a child. Teenagers quickly realize the romantic view of parenthood was more a television phenomenon than a reality because parenting is demanding and requires a level of emotional and spiritual maturity that many of them have not reached. Borrowing from Sigmund Freud, this may be called "privileged irresponsibility."

Inasmuch as teenage pregnancy is an epidemic problem in the black community, every black church needs a comprehensive Family Life program to assist in training, nurturing, encouraging, and teaching teenagers (male and females) about responsible relationships that begin with thinking well of themselves and respecting others. Before there can be any substantive social change in society, black youth must develop a positive self-esteem that will manifest itself in a reversal of some of the current trends and practices in the church and the community.

Martin Luther King, Jr.

After being thrust into the limelight as the leader of the Civil Rights movement during the 1950s and 1960s, Martin Luther King, Jr., can only be described in the language of Carl Jung as an *extraverted thinking type*.[16] His careful planning of the method for implementing nonviolent resistance, which required a signed pledge by each participant to abide by prescribed guidelines, demonstrates the extent to which King had thought about the procedure for bringing about justice and equality. Although his speeches were passionately delivered and his sermons drew tears, applause, and exuberant shouts of joy, his basic approach to obliterating injustice in the land was cognitive. Jung points out that the "actions of the extravert are recognizably related to external conditions. Inasmuch as they are not merely reactive to environment stimuli, they have a character that is always adapted to the actual circumstances . . ."[17]

Adaptation to circumstances has been the mark of black survival, through slavery and Jim Crow laws to the present. Indeed, the circumstances that surrounded King as leader of the black movement were always in such a state of flux that adjustment or adaptation to the external environment was frequent and necessary in order to maintain some degree of sanity or equilibrium between self-esteem and externally imposed degradation. The external condition of blacks caused King to be arrested and jailed twenty-nine times between 1956 and 1964.

In reference to the extraverted thinking type, Jung states that

> his moral code forbids him to tolerate exceptions; his idea must under all circumstances be realized, for in his eyes it is the purest conceivable formulation of objective reality and therefore must also be a universally valid truth quite indispensable for the salvation of mankind. This is not from any great love for his neighbor, but from the higher standpoint of justice and truth.[18]

Jung seems to elevate and isolate love from justice and truth here. However, we contend that the nexus between these three concepts is so intricate that the reality of their status as independent virtues, with no connection to the other, is very unlikely. Consequently, love in its truest form, with God as its symbol, is difficult to envision when isolated from justice and truth. This is the essence of Paul Tillich's argument in his book, *Love, Power, and Justice*.[19]

King as a Paradigm of Self-esteem

King was certainly a fighter for justice and a proponent of establishing the legal and ethical acknowledgment of the humanity of all people. Although his systematic approach to bringing forth justice in the land through love required a thinking attitude, its aim was to appeal to the feelings of the perpetrators of injustice. Teaching the participants to love their enemy, to refrain from violence, to sacrifice their lives for the freedom of all people was the core of the nonviolent movement. The concept of nonviolence gave rise to social reform and new public policy regarding the civil rights of blacks. Only a clear understanding of the self could allow King to continue and prevail during a very difficult struggle.

King can be described basically as an extraverted thinking type; however, he was not without feeling. He enjoyed playing with his children and listening to opera. Jung maintains that activities depending on feelings are repressed in this type. But it is possible that such repression is necessary in order to attain objective goals for the group. The feelings expressed by King, for example, toward his children in the limited amount of free time that he could savor do not merit characterizing him as the feeling type. Although his capacity for feeling is exemplified in his treatment of his children as well as in his soul-stirring speeches, his overall life was characteristically "extraverted/thinking." "Feeling" as an auxiliary function is characteristic of this type. However, King's life reflected the thinker, the theologian/philosopher, and preacher that he was trained to be. In this connection, the social condition, with its evils and guardians of evil, contributed to King's quest for social change. The external world with all of its problems, inequities, and injustices occupied an extremely significant part of his relatively brief existence. On the day of his death, at age thirty-nine, he was still engrossed in persuading many of his close assistants and followers of the merits of nonviolence.

It cannot be overemphasized that the concept of nonviolence required discipline and philosophical rationale. The posture of the oppressed seldom influences the reaction of the oppressor in the wake of historically ingrained feelings of superiority and power that are given status through laws and custom. Because of this, violence often erupted during the nonviolent protests. People were arrested because they were nonviolently in defiance of laws that perpetrated violence upon the human character of blacks and other active sympathizers. To practice nonviolence in the face of violent and debased treatment is a clear indication of self-control for the purpose of achieving a higher moral goal, the attainment of a collective freedom.

Although the extraverted thinking type generally can be described as appearing cold and impersonal, we have seen that this was not the case with King. The fact that he was able to lead an organization in the face of extreme difficulties and personal sacrifices demonstrates that he was not only committed and determined, but also self-assured and convinced that moral rightness is inherently powerful and transformational.

King as a Symbol of Leadership

King was the actual and perceived leader of black people during much of the Civil Rights struggle. He was drafted to head the Montgomery Improvement Association and later the Southern Christian Leadership Conference. He rose to prominence because the situation demanded it. King's capacity for leadership transcended the willingness to serve in time of crisis and was manifested in his ability to create the occasion for transforming the status quo into a liberation event. "The genius of the great leader lies in his apprehension of what times require and in carrying through in the teeth of great opposition an act that changes the times."[20] The time was right for him because he made it right; because he was able to meet the demands of the times. His articulate and inspiring oratory captured the hearts of young and old, black and white, rich and poor, lettered and unlettered. For blacks, he was a symbol and perpetrator of deliverance— the spark that kindled a flame of hope in the hearts and minds of those who had become resigned to *de facto* and *de jure* segregation and other blatant forms of inhuman ideologies and practices.

King was also a clergyman, a role which he played in his earlier capacity as pastor as well as in his later role as leader of the black people. His was a caring and compassionate character, and the religious themes of love, peace, justice, and suffering were plainly evidenced by his life. His life reflected his own sense of self-esteem. This becomes apparent in the way, before his assassination, he addressed a crowd of two thousand supporters:

> We've got some difficult days ahead. But it really doesn't matter with me now. Because I've been to the mountaintop—I won't mind. Like anybody, I would like to live a long life. Longevity has its place. But I am not concerned about that now. I just want to do God's will. And He's allowed me to go up to the mountain. And I've looked over and I have seen the promised land. I may not get there with you, but I want you to know tonight that we as a people will get to the Promised Land. So I'm happy tonight. I'm not fearing any man. Mine eyes have seen the glory of the coming of the Lord.[21]

King is essentially expressing his feeling of being in harmony with himself and the world. His words reflect a sense of unity and self-realization as well as extreme inner perception and direction. The sense of bodily death lurks in the terseness of his language, yet there is also life and peace in his words. His struggles, visions, and hopes seem to be less burdensome—he seems to be free from the worry and pain of struggling for the things to which he devoted his life. His words have such a ring of finality that each staccato sentence summarizes the unity of his life's work—unity symbolized by the reconciliation of the dichotomies of joy and sorrow, love and hate, violence and nonviolence, justice and injustice.

Finally, King was always faced with what he perceived as the greatest myth that white America espoused—that time would ease the pain of injustice.[22] He was convinced that time has only prolonged the "agony of injustice" and created despair in the *Sitz im Leben* of black people. In an effort to diffuse the "myth of time," King sought to change the structure of the dynamics of injustice and oppression by forcing society to acknowledge the ontology of black people and give credibility to his analysis of the existential situation of unfreedom that was endemic to the life of blacks.

King was a man the world often viewed as possessed by the quest for social and racial equality. However, he was human, which means that he was a man of balance—a man of turmoil and peace, joy and sorrow, frustration and serenity, who faced life with love and hope. Young people today need to aspire to become leaders in the tradition of King, because his life serves to remind them of the value of responsibility, education, family, church, community, social justice, and positive self-esteem.

Positive self-esteem is not only important in the life of the black church and community, but also brings our discussion full circle. If the black community and the church are to make a real difference in changing the conditions of our society, then the development of positive self-esteem within every individual in the church and community is a necessary prerequisite. Black people need to think of themselves as change agents with the potential to make a difference. Children need to be taught self-respect, and parents need to focus on enriching their lives and the lives of their nuclear and extended family members by whatever means available. For example, siblings will need to help each other read and write and spend time together in activities that will foster belief in their ability and potential.

Moreover, the black church and community need to turn the tide and redirect the energy and resources of the black community toward self-development. In addition, the millions of blacks who have immortalized Martin Luther King, Jr., need to reflect on his teachings and begin to emulate him in word and deed. When this happens, liberation and social change will begin to occur and the black church and black community can move toward a common goal of liberating themselves from the internal and external forces of oppression. This is the fullest form of evangelization because it brings transformation!

Notes

1: Blacks, Evangelicalism and Beyond

1. Carter G. Woodson, *The History of the Negro Church,* 2nd ed. (Washington, D.C., The Associated Publishing, 1945), 279.

2. Ibid., 279.

3. See Donald W. Dayton, "The Radical Message of Evangelical Christianity," in William K. Tabb, ed. *Churches in Struggle* (New York: Monthly Review Press, 1986)

4. James H. Cone, *For My People* (Maryknoll, N.Y.: Orbis Books, 1985), 120.

5. Ronald H. Nash, *Evangelicals in America* (Nashville: Abingdon Press, 1987), 23.

6. Ibid., 23.

7. Ibid., 27.

8. See Donald W. Dayton, *Discovering an Evangelical Heritage* (San Francisco: Harper & Row, 1976).

9. Ibid., 29.

10. Richard John Neuhaus, *The Naked Public Square* (Grand Rapids: Wm. B. Eerdmans, 1984), 10.

11. Ibid., 11.

12. Ibid., 89.

13. Ronald J. Sider, "An Evangelical Theology of Liberation," in *Perspectives on Evangelical Theology,* ed. Kenneth Kantzer and Stanley N. Gundry (Grand Rapids: Baker Book House, 1979), 131ff.

14. J. Lawrence Burkholder, "Popular Evangelicalism: An Appraisal" in *Evangelicalism and Anabaptism,* ed. C. Norman Kraus (Scottsdale, Pa.: Herald Press, 1979), 72.

15. Wes Michaelson, "Evangelicalism and Radical Discipleship," in *Evangelicalism and Radical Discipleship*, ed. C. Norman Kraus (Scottsdale, Pa.: Herald Press, 1979), 72.

16. Concerned Evangelicals, *Evangelical Witness in South Africa* (Grand Rapids: Wm. B. Eerdmans, 1986), 37.

17. Ibid., 30.

18. Ibid., 32.

19. James H. Cone, *God of the Oppressed* (New York: Seabury Press, 1975).

20. See H. Richard Niebuhr, *Christ and Culture* (New York: Harper & Brothers, 1951), where he discusses the subject of Augustine, Bishop of Hippo. Chap. 6 is especially helpful because its title, "Christ the Transformer of Culture," speaks specifically to our hypothesis that Jesus and the message of the Gospels suggest that we not fit into society as it is, but that social transformation is justified.

21. See Peter Paris, *The Social Teachings of the Black Churches* (Philadelphia: Fortress Press, 1985) for a thorough explanation of some of these teachings.

22. Marshall McLuhan, *Understanding Media* (New York: McGraw-Hill, 1964), 127.

23. See Reinhold Niebuhr, *The Nature and Destiny of Man*, vol. 1 (New York: Charles Scribner's Sons, 1941). Niebuhr discusses the concept of self and pride.

24. This information is from the ABC News program "Nightline," November 1980, hosted by Ted Koppel.

25. Peter Galuszka, "Moral Majority's Influence Disputed," *The Virginian-Pilot*, November 11, 1980, p. A4.

26. See chap. 1, "It Began Here," in S. Morris Engel, *The Study of Philosophy* (New York: Holt Rinehart & Winston, 1981). Also see Peter Odegrad, *Political Power and Social Change* (New Brunswick, N.J.: Rutgers University Press, 1966), esp. chap. 1, "No Single Thing Abides."

27. See the sources cited in n. 23 to understand in more detail Parmenides' notion that change is an illusion.

28. The fleeting nature of experience is indicated in the first three verses of Ecclesiastes (1:1-3); however, 1:4-11 suggest that the world is in constant motion but in the end there is nothing really new.

29. J. Deotis Roberts, *A Black Political Theology* (Philadelphia: Westminster Press, 1975), 124.

30. See Karl Marx's concept of "alienation" regarding the proletariat and the bourgeoisie in his *Communist Manifesto* (Karl Marx and Frederick Engels, *Manifesto of the Communist Party* [Chicago: C. H. Kerr Pub. Co., 1978]). Some whites in America feel alienated from the wielders of power. However, blacks are totally alienated socially, politically, and economically from the mainstream.

31. Martin Luther King, Jr., "An Address before the National Press Club," in James M. Washington, ed., *A Testament of Hope: The Essential Writings of Martin Luther King, Jr.* (San Francisco: Harper & Row, 1986), 104.

32. See Ernst Käsemann, *Jesus Means Freedom* (Philadelphia: Fortress Press, 1972).

33. Daniel Migliore, *Called To Freedom: Liberation Theology and the Future of Christian Doctrine* (Philadelphia: Fortress Press, 1980), 27.

34. See Martin Hengel, *Christ and Power* (Philadelphia: Fortress Press, 1977), 20.

35. James Childress and John Macquarie, eds., *The Westminster Dictionary of Christian Ethics* (Philadelphia: Westminster Press, 1986), 238.

36. James H. Cone, *God of the Oppressed* (New York: The Seabury Press, 1975), 10.

37. The song "This Joy I Have" belongs to the public domain and is often heard in the black church under different arrangements. In Mt. Pleasant Baptist Church, Norfolk, Va., Sister Mildred Bright, a member of the senior choir, often led this gospel-style song.

38. Jens Glebe-Möller, *A Political Dogmatic* (Philadelphia: Fortress Press, 1987), 117.

39. James H. Cone, "The Gospel of Jesus, Black People, and Black Power," in *Border Regions of Faith: An Anthology of Religion and Social Change*, ed. Kenneth Aman (Maryknoll, N.Y.: Orbis Books, 1987), 154.

40. Glebe-Möller, *Political Dogmatic*, 119.

41. See Jürgen Moltmann, *A Passion for Life* (Philadelphia: Fortress Press, 1976).

42. Adolf Harnack, *What Is Christianity?* (New York: Harper & Row, 1957), 101.

43. For a thorough treatment of this subject, see Sar Levitan and Isaac Shapiro, *Working But Poor: America's Contradiction* (Baltimore: Johns Hopkins University Press, 1987).

44. Jon Sobrino, *Jesus in Latin America* (Maryknoll, N.Y.: Orbis Books, 1987), 13.

45. See Walter A. Elwell, ed., *Evangelical Dictionary of Theology* (Grand Rapids: Baker Book House, 1984), 379.

46. Roberts, *Black Political Theology*.

47. Cone, *For My People*, 115–16.

2: The Urban Community

1. Samuel D. Proctor, *Preaching About Crisis in the Community*, esp. chap. 6, "The Good News and the Quest for Community" (Philadelphia: Westminster Press, 1988).

2. Dietrich Bonhoeffer, *Life Together* (New York: Harper, 1954), 21.

3. Proctor, 95.

4. Reinhold Niebuhr, *The Nature and Destiny of Man*, vol. 1 (New York: C. Scribners Sons, 1941).

5. Robert Ringer, *Looking Out for Number One* (Beverly Hills, Calif.: Los Angeles Book Corp.; New York: Funk & Wagnalls, 1977).

6. Karl Marx, "Contribution to the Critique of Hegel's Philosophy of Right: Introduction," in Karl Marx and Friedrich Engels, *On Religion*, ed. Reinhold

Niebuhr (New York: Shocken Books, Inc., 1964; reprint: Chico, Calif.: Scholars Press, 1982), 42.

7. Gayraud Wilmore, *Black Religion and Black Radicalism* (Garden City, N.Y.: Doubleday & Co., Inc., 1972), 187–227.

8. See "Ten Religious Groups with Biggest Black Membership, *Ebony* (March 1984), 142.

9. Ibid.

10. Ibid.

11. C. G. Jung, *Psychological Types* (Princeton, N.J.: Princeton University Press, 1971), 389.

12. Hendrikus Berkhof, *The Doctrine of the Holy Spirit* (Atlanta: John Knox Press, 1976), 34.

13. E. Franklin Frazier, *The Negro Church in America* (New York: Schocken Books, 1963), 34–35.

14. Joseph R. Washington, Jr., *Black Sects and Cults: The Power Axis in the Ethnic Ethic* (Garden City, N.Y.: Doubleday Anchor Books, 1973), 57.

15. Ibid.

16. See Langston Hughes's epic poem, "Refugee in America" *(Saturday Evening Post* 215 [6 Feb. 1943]:64), where he describes the state of being black with masterful poetic rhyme and reason.

17. More writers have talked about this concept since DuBois; however, all of them have acknowledged the fact that DuBois is the father of this terminology. Geneva Smitherman, Peter Paris, and several others have made specific reference to the concept "double-consciousness." I have used the word "ambivalent" to reflect the same phenomenon.

18. Geneva Smitherman, *Talking and Testifying* (Boston: Houghton Mifflin, 1977), 10–11.

19. For a more thorough analysis of ambivalence, see chap. 3 in James H. Harris, *Black Ministers and Laity in the Urban Church* (Lanham, Md.: University Press of America, 1987). This chapter is an attempt to explain the results of my research on laity expectations of clergy where the sample expected the minister to give priority to evangelistic efforts while simultaneously giving precedence to the eradication of oppression and injustice in society. This chapter, "Ambivalence among Clergy and Laity," should be helpful in providing more understanding of the concept.

20. Peter Paris, *The Social Teaching of the Black Churches* (Philadelphia: Fortress Press, 1985), 76.

21. Ibid.

22. See James M. Washington, ed. *A Testament of Hope: The Essential Writings of Martin Luther King, Jr.* (San Francisco: Harper & Row, 1986), for an anthology of King's writings. Moreover, this letter appears in many books on philosophy and social ethics.

23. David Clarebout, *Urban America* (Grand Rapids: Zondervan, 1983), 17–18.

24. Katherine Bradbury, et al., *Urban Decline and the Future of America's Cities* (Washington: Brookings Institution, 1982), 18.

25. Ibid.

26. Ibid., 24.

27. Ibid., 25.

28. Ibid.

29. Ibid.

30. Duncan Timms, *The Urban Mosaic: Toward a Theory of Residential Differentiation* (Cambridge, Mass.: Cambridge University Press, 1971), 211.

31. Ibid., 99.

32. Ibid., 101.

33. Herbert Hill, "Demographic Change and Racial Ghettos: The Crisis of American Cities," reprinted from *Journal of American Law* 44 (Winter 1966).

34. See Peter Steinfels, *The Neoconservatives: The Men Who Are Changing America's Politics* (New York: Simon & Schuster, 1979), for more details on this subject.

35. Nathan Glazer, "The Limits of Social Policy," in *Commentary* (Sept. 1971), 51–58.

36. United States Commission on Civil Rights, *Affirmative Action in the 1980s: Dismantling the Process of Discrimination* (Washington, D.C.: Clearinghouse Pub. 70), Nov. 1981, 1.

37. George Gilder, *Wealth and Poverty* (New York: Basic Books, 1981).

38. Nathan Glazer, *Affirmative Discrimination* (New York: Basic Books, 1975).

39. See A. Leon Higginbotham, *In the Matter of Color: The Colonial Period* (New York: Oxford University Press, 1978), and Albert J. Raboteau, *Slave Religion: The Invisible Institution in the Antebellum South* (New York: Oxford University Press, 1978), for an excellent explication of the experience of blacks in America.

40. Martin Luther King, Jr., "Letter from Birmingham Jail," in *Why We Can't Wait* (New York: Harper & Row, 1963), 92, and also in Washington, *A Testament of Hope,* 300.

41. Joseph R. Washington, Jr. ed., *Black Religion and Public Policy: Ethical and Historical Perspectives* (n.p., 1978) (Edited papers of a symposium on the function of black religion in public policy held at the University of Pennsylvania under the sponsorship of Afro American Studies Program, March 1978).

42. Sar Levitan and Isaac Shapiro, *Working But Poor: America's Contradiction* (Baltimore: Johns Hopkins University Press, 1987).

43. For a more detailed discussion, see David Roberts, *Victorian Origins of the Welfare State,* 1960, and Stephen Marcus, "Their Brother's Keepers: An Episode from English History," in *Doing Good: The Limits of Benevolence,* ed. Willard Gaylin, Ira Glasser, Steven Marcus, and David J. Rothman (New York: Pantheon Books, 1978).

3: Black Theology

1. As a postdoctoral fellow at United Theological Seminary, Dayton, Ohio, I have discussed this topic with Dr. Samuel Proctor, who is my mentor. In these

discussions, class lectures, and in reviewing this manuscript, Dr. Proctor has expressed this sentiment.

2. James H. Cone, *For My People: Black Theology and the Black Church* (New York: Orbis Books, 1984), 117.

3. Cone, in *A Black Theology of Liberation* (New York: J. B. Lippincott, 1970) lists six sources of black theology: black experience, black history, black culture, revelation, Scripture, and tradition (53–74).

4. Ibid., 59.

5. Gayraud Wilmore, *Black Religion and Black Radicalism* (New York: Doubleday & Co., 1973).

6. Most black theologians are committed to the church and its role in the development of black theology. Professor Wilmore has been a leader in this regard.

7. Cone, *For My People,* 117.

8. Jens Glebe-Möller, *A Political Dogmatic* (Philadelphia: Fortress Press, 1987), 67.

9. See Allan Aubrey Boesak, *Farewell to Innocence* (New York: Orbis Books, 1976), esp. chap. 1, "On Theology," which is basically an analysis of black theology.

10. These persons (along with others) have written systematically on this subject and have developed black theology as it is known today. For example, besides *For My People* and *A Black Theology of Liberation,* see these books by James H. Cone: *Black Theology and Black Power* (San Francisco: Harper & Row, 1989); *The Spirituals and the Blues* (New York: Seabury Press, 1972); *God of the Oppressed* (New York: Seabury Press, 1975). In addition to his classic *Black Religion and Black Radicalism,* Gayraud Wilmore's *Black Theology: A Documentary History, 1966–1979* (New York: Orbis Books, 1979), edited with James Cone, provides an excellent foundation for understanding black liberation theology. Other notable works include J. Deotis Roberts, *Liberation and Reconciliation: A Black Theology* (Philadelphia: Westminster Press, 1971); and *Black Theology in Dialogue* (Philadelphia: Westminster Press, 1987); Major J. Jones, *Black Awareness: A Theology of Hope* (Nashville: Abingdon Press, 1971); *Christian Ethics for Black Theology* (Nashville: Abingdon, 1974); and *The Color of God: The Concept of God in Afro-American Thought* (Macon, Ga.: Mercer University Press, 1974). Albert Cleage was one of the early interpreters of black theology; his *Black Messiah* (New York: Sheed & Ward, 1968) is a vital part of the literature. Joseph Washington, in *Black Religion: The Negro and Christianity in the United States* (Boston: Beacon Press, 1964); *The Politics of God* (Boston: Beacon Press, 1967); and *Black Sects and Cults: The Power Axis in the Ethnic Ethic* (Garden City, N.Y.: Doubleday Anchor Books, 1975) have contributed enormously to the understanding of black theology.

11. Wilmore and Cone, eds., *Black Theology: A Documentary History,* 101.

12. See Wilmore, *Black Religion and Black Radicalism,* 295, and John C. Bennett, "Black Theology of Liberation," in *Black Theology: A Documentary History,* ed. Wilmore and Cone.

13. Boesak, *Farewell to Innocence,* 18.

14. Cone, "The White Church and Black Power," in *Black Theology: A Documentary History,* ed. Wilmore and Cone, 113.

15. Cone, *God of the Oppressed,* 138.

16. Wilmore, *Black Religion and Black Radicalism,* 297.

17. Jones, *The Color of God,* 6.

18. Ibid., 6–7.

19. Cone, *A Black Theology of Liberation,* 23.

20. See Wilmore and Cone, eds., *Black Theology: A Documentary History.*

21. Jones, *The Color of God,* 6.

22. Roberts, *Black Theology in Dialogue,* 117.

23. See Leonardo Boff and Clodovis Boff, *Introducing Liberation Theology* (Maryknoll, N.Y.: Orbis Books, 1987). They discuss three meditations: socioanalytical mediation, hermeneutical mediation, and practical mediation. Each of these three mediations is related to the larger issue of doing liberation theology. The socioanalytical mediation tries to discover what God is saying to the poor and practical mediation makes an effort to determine what can be done according to God's Word to change the situation.

24. Jesse Jackson, "Common Ground and Common Sense," *Vital Speeches of the Day* 54 (15 Aug. 1988): 649–53.

25. Cone, *God of the Oppressed,* 152.

26. Cone, *For My People,* 99.

4: Church Administration

1. Floyd Massey, Jr. and Samuel B. McKinney, *Church Administration in the Black Perspective* (Valley Forge, Pa.: Judson Press, 1976).

2. C. Eric Lincoln, *The Black Church Since Frazier* (New York: Schocken Books, 1974), 135.

3. Ibid., 136.

4. Martin Luther King, Jr., "I Have a Dream," in *A Testament of Hope: The Essential Writings of Martin Luther King, Jr.,* ed. James M. Washington (San Francisco: Harper & Row, 1987), 217–20.

5. Hiawatha Bray, "A Separate Altar: Distinctions of the Black Church," *Christianity Today* (September 19, 1986), 21.

6. Ibid., 22.

7. Ibid., 23.

8. Randall Frame, "The Cost of Being Black: Out of Work, Out of Money and Out of Favor—A Culture At Risk," *Christianity Today,* (September 19, 1986), 19.

9. Daniel L. Migliore, *Called to Freedom: Liberation Theology and the Future of Christian Doctrine* (Philadelphia: Westminster Press, 1980), 56–57.

10. George A. Buttrick, ed., *The Interpreter's Bible* (Nashville: Abingdon Press, 1951), 7:280.

11. James D. Williams, ed., *The State of Black America* (New York: National Urban League, 1982), 233.

12. James Gustafson and James T. Laney, eds., *On Being Responsible: Issues in Personal Ethics* (New York: Harper & Row, 1968), 299.

13. Joseph R. Washington, Jr., *Black Sects and Cults: The Power Axis in the Ethnic Ethic* (Garden City, N.Y.: Doubleday Anchor Books, 1973), 57.

14. See James Cone, "New Roles in the Ministry: A Theological Appraisal," in *Black Theology: A Documentary History 1966–1979*, ed. Gayraud S. Wilmore and James A. Cone (New York: Orbis Books, 1979), 389.

15. James H. Harris, "Laity Expectations of Clergy in the Black Urban Church," (Ph.D. diss., Old Dominion University, 1985).

16. Sar Levitan and Isaac Shapiro, *Working But Poor: America's Contradiction* (Baltimore: Johns Hopkins University Press, 1987).

17. See "America's Hidden Poor," *U.S. News and World Report* (Jan. 11, 1988), 18–24.

18. Levitan and Shapiro, *Working But Poor,* 15–16.

19. Michael Harrington, *The New American Poverty* (New York: Penguin Books, 1984), 15.

20. Ibid.

21. William Ouchi, *Theory Z* (New York: Avon Books, 1981), 4.

22. Samuel Proctor is my major professor in a program leading to a D. Min. in Preaching at United Theological Seminary in Dayton, Ohio. This is a paraphrase of notes taken from one of his lectures in spring 1990.

23. Ouchi, *Theory Z,* 5.

24. H. Beecher Hicks, *Images of the Black Preacher* (Valley Forge, Pa.: Judson Press, 1977).

25. Ouchi, *Theory Z,* 6.

26. Douglas McGregor, *The Human Side of Enterprise* (New York: McGraw-Hill, 1960).

27. For more information on popular management theories and practices see Thomas J. Peters and Robert H. Waterman, Jr., *In Search of Excellence* (New York: Warner Books, 1984); Tom Peters and Nancy Austin, *A Passion for Excellence* (New York: Random House, 1985); Kenneth Blanchard and Spencer Johnson, *The One Minute Manager* (New York: William Morrow, 1982); and John Naisbitt, *Megatrends* (New York: Warner Books, 1982).

28. See David R. Morgan, *Managing Urban America* (North Scituate, Mass.: Duxbury Press, 1979), 197.

29. Ibid.

30. Ibid., 198.

31. Paul Wehr, *Conflict Regulation* (Boulder, Colo.: Westview Press, 1979).

32. Ibid., 58.

33. Ibid., 59.

34. Ibid., 61.

5: Worship and Preaching

1. James H. Cone, *Speaking the Truth* (Grand Rapids: Wm. B. Eerdmans, 1986), 139.

2. William Ryan, *Blaming the Victim* (New York: Pantheon Books, 1971).

3. Kenneth Clark, "The Power of the Church," in *The Black Church in America,* ed. Hart Nelson, Raytha L. Yolkey, and Anne K. Nelson (New York: Basic Books, 1971), 143–49.

4. Wyatt Tee Walker, *Somebody's Calling My Name* (Valley Forge, Pa.: Judson Press, 1979), 24.

5. Ibid.

6. Ibid., 26.

7. Portia K. Maultsby, "The Use and Performance of Hymnody, Spirituals, and Gospels in the Black Church," *The Journal of the Interdenominational Theological Center* 14 (Fall 1986/Spring 87): 156–57.

8. This gospel song, "We Need to Hear from You," by Sandra Crouch, is a staple in the black church today. Its soft and melodious sound is prayerful and comforting when following or preceding a prayer. Its meditative quality is very meaningful in worship.

9. The old Negro spiritual is still used in the black worship service and shows the relationship that blacks have with the Old Testament struggles of the Israelites.

10. See 1 Cor. 2:4. However, see also John Mason Stapleton, *Preaching in Demonstration of the Spirit and Power* (Philadelphia: Fortress Press, 1988).

11. Edward Mote, "My Hope Is Built on Nothing Less," cited from *Lutheran Book of Worship* (Minneapolis: Augsburg, 1978), 293, 294.

12. Henry Mitchell, *The Recovery of Preaching* (San Francisco: Harper & Row, 1977), 54.

6: Christian Education

1. J. Deotis Roberts, *Black Theology in Dialogue* (Philadelphia: Westminster Press, 1987), 117.

2. Shirley A. Chisholm, "Black Religion and Education," in *Black Religion and Public Policy: Ethical and Historical Perspectives,* ed. Joseph R. Washington, Jr. (U.S.A.: Joseph R. Washington, Jr. Pub., 1978), 41–45.

3. Paulo Freire, *Pedagogy of the Oppressed* (New York: Seabury Press, 1973), and *Education for Critical Consciousness* (New York: Continuum, 1973).

4. Interview and questionnaire from Rev. Thomas Smith, Pittsburgh, Pa.

5. The history and other information about Canaan Baptist Church was sent to me at my request. This information is based on those documents. Dr. Walker's staff was unable to arrange a telephone interview or a written response to a questionnaire.

6. Alex Poinsett, "Suffer the Little Children," in *Ebony* (August 1988), 144.

7. Norfolk, Virginia adopted a plan to reduce crosstown busing for purposes of desegregation in the elementary schools. After years of litigation the 4th Circuit Court of Appeals in Richmond, Va. upheld the lower court's decision that such a plan was not in violation of the law. During this period, the writer was president of a citizen-based group opposing the school board's efforts to reduce busing for the purpose of desegregation. Inasmuch as the school board's decision was upheld,

Norfolk now has ten elementary schools that have become essentially resegregated. See *Riddick, et al. v. Norfolk School Board, et al.*

8. See for example, Christopher Jencks, *Inequality: A Reassessment of the Effect of Family and Schooling in America* (New York: Harper & Row, 1972), James Coleman, *The Adolescent Society* (New York: Free Press, 1961), Arthur Jensen, "How Much Can We Boost IQ and Scholastic Achievement?" *Harvard Educational Review* 39 (1969): 1–123, 449–83, and Michael Rutter et al., *Fifteen Thousand Hours: Secondary Schools and Their Effects on Children* (Cambridge, Mass.: Harvard University Press, 1979). For more information on educational reform, see Ronald Edmonds, "Some Schools Work and Others Can," *Social Policy* 9 (1979): 28–32, and Marilyn Gittell, Maurice Berube, and Mario Fantini, *Decentralization: Achieving Reform* (New York: Praeger, 1973).

9. See John Dewey, *Experience and Education* (New York: Macmillan Publishers, 1938); Lawrence A. Cremin, *Public Education* (New York: Basic Books, 1976); and John Dewey's major work, *Democracy and Education* (New York: Macmillan Publishers, 1916).

10. John U. Ogbu, *Minority Education and Caste: The American System in Cross-Cultural Perspective* (New York: Academic Press, Inc., 1978), 22–23.

11. Ibid., 23.

12. Ibid., 132.

13. Ibid.

14. Sid Smith, *Ten Super Sunday Schools in the Black Community* (Nashville: Broadman Press, 1986).

15. See James H. Cone, *For My People: Black Theology and the Black Church* (New York: Orbis Books, 1984), 115, where he quotes James S. Tinney, "The Moral Majority: Operating Under the Hood of Religious Rights," from *Dollars and Sense* (July 1981). In referring to the Moral Majority, Cone describes their practices as "blatant racist Christianity."

16. See Mary Love, "Musings on Sunday School in the Black Community," in *Renewing the Sunday School,* ed. D. Campbell Wyckoff (Birmingham, Ala.: Religious Education Press, 1986), 162.

17. *The Kairos Document, Challenge to the Church: A Theological Comment on the Political Crisis in South Africa* (Grand Rapids, Mich.: Wm. B. Eerdmans, 1986), 25.

18. See James D. Tyms, "The Black Church, Black Religious Experience, Roots for the Future," in *To You Who Teach in the Black Church,* ed. Riggins R. Earl (Nashville: National Baptist Publishing Board, 1972), 117.

7: Self-esteem in the Black Church

1. See Abram Kardiner and Lionel Oversey, *The Mark of Oppression: Explorations in the Personality of the American Negro* (New York: World Publishing, Meridian Books, 1951). Also note the introduction, Kenneth and Mamie Clark, "What Do Blacks Think of Themselves?" *Ebony* (November 1980), 176ff.

2. Karl A. Menninger, *Man Against Himself* (New York: Harcourt, Brace & World, 1938), 4.

3. Ibid., 5.

4. See Norman O. Brown, *Life Against Death: The Psycho-Analytical Meaning of History,* 2d ed. (Middletown, Conn.: Wesleyan University Press, 1985). He discusses Freud's two instincts, Eros and Death, in great detail. This work is laden with philosophical references and is an excellent supplementary source for strengthening one's understanding of Freud and Minninger.

5. Donald W. Felker, *Building Positive Self-Concepts* (Minneapolis: Burgess Publishing Company, 1974), 2.

6. See John Ogbu, *The Next Generation: An Ethnography of Education in an Urban Neighborhood* (New York: Academic Press, 1974).

7. Henry H. Mitchell and Nicholas Cooper Lewter, *Soul Theology: The Heart of American Black Culture* (San Francisco: Harper & Row, 1986), 46.

8. John R. W. Stott, "Am I Supposed to Love Myself or Hate Myself?" *Christianity Today* (April 20, 1984).

9. Felker, *Building Positive Self-Concepts,* 6.

10. See Shirley C. Samuel, *Enhancing Self-Concept in Early Childhood: Theory and Practice* (New York: Human Sciences Press, 1977), and Chad Gordon's *Looking Ahead: Self-Conceptions, Race and Family as Determinants of Adolescent Orientation to Achievement* (Washington, D.C.: American Sociological Association, 1972). These books are excellent repositories of information on self-concept and how it correlates with other variables.

11. See Ronald Edmonds, "Some Schools Work and More Can," *Social Policy* 9 (1979): 28–32.

12. Don E. Hamachek, *Encounters with the Self* (New York: Holt, Rinehart & Winston, 1978), 4.

13. James D. Williams, ed., *The State of Black America 1986* (New York: National Urban League, 1986), 65.

14. Ibid., 72.

15. Cheryl D. Hayes, ed., *Risking the Future: Adolescent Sexuality, Pregnancy and Childbearing* (Washington, D.C.: National Academy Press, 1987), 1:138–39.

16. Carl Jung, the noted Swiss-German psychoanalyst, in *Psychological Types* (Princeton, N.J.: Princeton University Press, 1971), 6:334. uses the word "extraverted" and spells it with an *a* as indicated. General American usage of the word is extroverted.

17. Ibid.

18. Ibid., 347.

19. Paul Tillich, *Love, Power, and Justice* (New York: Oxford University Press, 1954).

20. Lerone Bennett, *What Manner of Man* (New York: Johnson Publishing Company, 1986), 131.

21. Ibid., 240.

22. Martin Luther King, Jr., "Remaining Awake through a Great Revolution," in *A Testament of Hope: The Essential Writings of Martin Luther King, Jr.,* ed. James M. Washington (San Francisco: Harper & Row, 1986), 270.

Bibliography

Bachrach, Peter, and Morton S. Baratz. *Power and Poverty: Theory and Practice.* New York: Oxford University Press, 1970.

Bailey, Robert W. *New Ways in Christian Worship.* Nashville, Tenn.: Broadman Press, 1981.

Bennett, Lerone. *What Manner of Man.* New York: Johnson Publishing Company, 1968.

Bloesch, Donald G. *Essentials of Evangelical Theology.* San Francisco: Harper & Row, 1978.

Bray, Hiawatha. "A Separate Altar: Distinction of the Black Church." *Christianity Today*, September 19, 1986.

Brown, Norman O. *Life Against Death: The Psychoanalytical Meaning of History*, 2d ed. Middletown, Conn.: Wesleyan University Press, 1985.

Buttrick, Georg A., ed. *The Interpreter's Bible.* Vol. VII. Nashville: Abingdon Press, 1951.

Cassidy, Richard J. *Society and Politics in the Acts of the Apostles.* New York: Orbis Books, 1987.

Childs, John B. *The Political Black Minister: A Study in Afro-American Politics and Religion.* Boston, Mass.: G. K. Hall, 1988.

Clarke, John Henrik. *Marcus Garvey and the Vision of Africa.* New York: Random House, 1974.

Cobb, John B., Jr. *Liberal Christianity at the Crossroads.* Philadelphia: Westminster Press, 1973.

Concerned Evangelicals. *Evangelical Witness in South Africa.* Grand Rapids: Wm. B. Eerdmans, 1986.

Cone, James H. *A Black Theology of Liberation.* New York: J. B. Lippincott, 1970.

————. *For My People: Black Theology and the Black Church.* New York: Orbis Books, 1984.

————. *God of the Oppressed.* New York: Seabury Press, 1975.

————. *Speaking the Truth: Ecumenism, Liberation, and Black Theology.* Grand Rapids: Wm. B. Eerdmans, 1986.

————. *Black Theology: A Documentary History, 1966–1979.* Maryknoll, N.Y.: Orbis Books, 1979.

Davis, John J. *Foundations of Evangelical Theology.* Grand Rapids: Baker Book House, 1984.

Dean, Thomas, and John C. Raines, eds. *Marxism and Radical Religion: Essay Toward a Revolutionary Humanism.* Philadelphia: Temple University Press, 1970.

Dyer, William G. *Strategies for Managing Change.* Reading, Mass.: Addison-Wesley, 1984.

Edmonds, Ronald. "Some Schools Work and More Can," *Social Policy* 9 (March-April 1979): 28–32.

Efird, James M. *Jeremiah, Prophet Under Siege.* Valley Forge, Pa.: Judson Press, 1979.

Ellis, Marc H. *Toward a Jewish Theology of Liberation.* New York: Orbis Books, 1987.

Ellul, Jacques. *The Ethics of Freedom.* Translated and edited by Geoffrey W. Bromiley. Grand Rapids: Wm. B. Eerdmans, 1976.

Engel, S. Morris. *The Study of Philosophy.* New York: Holt, Rinehart & Winston, 1981.

Garvey, Marcus. *Philosophy and Opinions* or *Africa for the Africans.* Compiled by Amy Jacques Garvey, with an introduction by E. U. Essien-Udom. London: Frank Cass & Co., 1977.

Felker, Donald W. *Building Positive Self-Concepts.* Minneapolis: Burgress Publishing Co., 1974.

Frame, Randall. "The Cost of Being Black: Out of Work, Out of Money and Out of Favor—A Culture at Risk." *Christianity Today,* September 19, 1986.

Frazier, E. Franklin. *The Negro Church in America.* New York: Schocken Books, 1963.

————. *The Negro Family in the United States.* Chicago: University of Chicago Press, 1966.

Freire, Paulo. *Pedagogy of the Oppressed.* New York: Seabury Press, 1973.

Galuska, Peter. "Moral Majority's Influence Disputed." *The Virginian-Pilot,* November 11, 1980.

Gamson, William A. *The Strategy of Social Protest.* Homewood, Ill.: Dorsey Press, 1975.

Gaylin, Willard, I. Glasser, S. Marcuss, and D. J. Rothman. *Doing Good: The Limits of Benevolence.* New York: Pantheon Books, 1981.

Goode, Erich. *Social Class and Church Participation.* New York: Arno Press, 1980.

Gordon, Chad. *Looking Ahead: Self Conceptions, Race and Family as Determinants of Adolescent Orientation to Achievement.* Washington, D.C.: American Sociological Association, 1972.

Gottwald, Norman K. *The Bible and Liberation: Political and Social Hermeneutics.* New York: Orbis Books, 1983.

Gustafson, James, and James T. Laney, eds. *On Being Responsible: Issues in Personal Ethics.* New York: Harper & Row, 1968.

Gutierrez, Gustavo. *A Theology of Liberation.* New York: Orbis Books, 1980.

Hamachek, Don E. *Encounters with the Self,* 2d ed. New York: Holt, Rinehart & Winston, 1978.

Hamilton, Charles V. *The Black Preacher in America.* New York: William Morrow, 1972.

Harnack, Adolf. *What Is Christianity?* New York: Harper & Row, 1957.

Harrell, David Edwin, Jr. *Varieties of Southern Evangelicalism.* Macon, Ga.: Mercer University Press, 1981.

Harrington, Michael. *The New American Poverty.* New York: Penguin Books, 1985.

Harris, James H. *Black Ministers and Laity in the Urban Church.* Lanham, Md.: University Press of America, 1987.

Hayes, Cheryl D., ed. *Risking the Future: Adolescent Sexuality, Pregnancy and Childbearing.* Vol. 1. Washington, D.C.: National Academy Press, 1987.

Hengel, Martin. *The Son of God.* Philadelphia: Fortress Press, 1976.

Hodgson, Peter C. *Children of Freedom: Black Liberation in Christian Perspective.* Philadelphia: Fortress Press, 1974.

Howard, Thomas. *Evangelical Is Not Enough.* Nashville: Thomas Nelson & Sons, 1984.

Hunter, James D. *American Evangelicalism: Conservative Religion and Quandary of Modernity.* New Brunswick, N.J.: Rutgers University Press, 1983.

Inch, Morris A. *The Evangelical Challenge.* Philadelphia: Westminster Press, 1978.

Jenkins, Adelbert H. *The Psychology of the Afro-American: A Humanistic Approach.* New York: Pergamon Press, 1982.

Jones, Amos, Jr. *Paul's Message of Freedom: What Does It Mean to the Black Church?* Valley Forge, Pa.: Judson Press, 1984.

Jones, Major J. *The Color of God: The Concept of God in Afro-American Thought.* Macon, Ga.: Mercer University Press, 1987.

Jordon, Winthrop. *The Whiteman's Burden: Historical Origins of Racism in the United States.* New York: Oxford University Press, 1974.

Jung, C. G. *Two Essays on Analytical Psychology.* New York: Bollinger Foundation, 1953.

Jung, C. G. *Psychological Types.* Princeton: Princeton University Press, 1971.

————. *The Kairos Document, Challenge to the Churches: A Theological Comment on the Political Crisis in South Africa.* Grand Rapids: Wm. B. Eerdmans, 1986.

Kantzer, Kenneth S., and Stanley N. Gundry. *Perspectives on Evangelical Theology.* Grand Rapids: Baker Book House, 1979.

Kardiner, Abram, M.D., and Lionel Oversey, M.D. *The Mark of Oppression: Explorations in the Personality of the American Negro.* New York: World Publishing, Meridian Books, 1951.

Käsemann, Ernst. *Jesus Means Freedom.* Philadelphia: Fortress Press, 1974.

King, Martin Luther, Jr. *Where Do We Go from Here: Chaos or Community?* Boston: Beacon Press, 1967.

Levitan, Sar A., and Isaac Shapiro. *Working But Poor: America's Contradiction.* Baltimore: Johns Hopkins University Press, 1987.

Lewter, Nicholas Cooper, and Henry Mitchell. *Soul Theology: The Heart of American Black Culture.* San Francisco: Harper & Row, 1986.

Lightner, Robert P. *Neoevangelical Today.* Nashville: Abingdon Press, 1978.

Lincoln, C. Eric. *The Black Church Since Frazier.* New York: Schocken Books, 1974.

————. *My Face Is Black.* Boston: Beacon Press, 1964.

Marable, Manning. *How Capitalism Underdeveloped Black America: Problems in Race, Political Economy and Society.* Boston: South End Press, 1983.

————. *Grassroots of America: Essays Toward Afro-American Liberation.* Boston: South End Press, 1980.

Massey, Floyd, Jr., and Samuel B. McKinney. *Church Administration in the Black Perspective.* Valley Forge, Pa.: Judson Press, 1976.

McLuhan, Marshall. *Understanding Media.* New York: McGraw-Hill, 1964.

Meier, Kenneth J. *Politics and the Bureaucracy.* Belmont, Calif.: Wadsworth Publishing Co., 1979.

————. *Politics and the Bureaucracy: Policymaking in the Fourth Branch of Government.* North Scituate, Mass.: Duxbury Press, 1979.

Menninger, Karl A. *Man Against Himself.* New York: Harcourt, Brace & World, 1938.

Migliore, Daniel L. *Called to Freedom: Liberation Theology and the Future of Christian Doctrine.* Philadelphia: Westminster Press, 1980.

Mitchell, Henry H., and Nicholas Cooper Lewter. *Soul Theology: The Heart of American Black Culture.* San Francisco: Harper & Row, 1986.

Moore, Wilbert E. *Social Change,* 2d ed. Englewood Cliffs, N.J.: Prentice-Hall, 1974.

Nash, Ronald H. *Evangelicals in America.* Nashville: Abingdon Press, 1987.

Neuhaus, Richard J. *The Naked Public Square: Religion and Democracy in America.* Grand Rapids: Wm. B. Eerdmans, 1984.

Neibuhr, H. Richard. *Christ and Culture.* New York: Harper & Brothers, 1951.

Neibuhr, Reinhold. *The Nature and Destiny of Man.* Vol. I. New York: Charles Scribner's Sons, 1941.

Odegard, Peter H. *Political Power & Social Change.* New Brunswick, N. J.: Rutgers University Press, 1966.

Paris, Peter. *The Social Teachings of the Black Churches.* Philadelphia: Fortress Press, 1985.

Parsons, Talcott. *Social Systems and the Evolution of Action Theory.* New York: Free Press, 1977.

Pitkin, Hanna Fenichel. *Wittgenstein and Justice.* Berkeley and Los Angeles: University of California Press, 1972.

Poloma, Margaret M. *The Charismatic Movement: Is There a New Pentecost?* Boston: G. K. Hall, 1981.

Quebedeaux, Richard. *The Young Evangelicals.* New York: Harper & Row, 1974.
Raines, John C., and Thomas Dean. *Marxism and Radical Religion.* Philadelphia: Temple University Press, 1970.
Reed, Adolph L., Jr. *The Jesse Jackson Phenomenon: The Crisis of Purpose in Afro-American Politics.* New Haven: Yale University Press, 1986.
Roberts, J. Deotis. *A Black Political Theology.* Philadelphia: Westminster Press, 1975.
————. *Black Theology in Dialogue.* Philadelphia: Westminster Press, 1987.
Roberts, Ron E. *Social Problems: Human Possibilities.* St. Louis: C. V. Mosby, 1978.
Samuel, Shirley C. *Enhancing Self-Concept in Early Childhood: Theory and Practice.* New York: Human Sciences Press, 1977.
Schaller, Lyle E. *The Change Agent.* Nashville: Abingdon Press, 1972.
Schuller, Robert H. *Self-Esteem—The New Reformation.* Waco, Tex.: Word Books, 1982.
Sider, Ronald J. *Evangelicals and Development: Toward a Theology of Social Change.* Philadelphia: Westminster Press, 1981.
Smitherman, Geneva. *Talking and Testifying.* Boston: Houghton Mifflin, 1977.
Sobrino, Jon. *Jesus in Latin America.* New York: Orbis Books, 1987.
Stein, Judith. *The World of Marcus Garvey: Race and Class in Modern Society.* Baton Rouge, La.: Louisiana State University Press, 1986.
Steiss, Alan Walter, John W. Dickey, Bruce Phelps, and Michael Harvey. *Dynamic Change and the Urban Ghetto.* Lexington, Mass.: D. C. Heath & Co., 1975.
Stott, John R. W. "Am I Supposed to Love Myself or Hate Myself?" *Christianity Today,* April 20, 1984.
Washington, James Melvin. *Frustrated Fellowship: The Black Baptist Quest for Social Power.* Macon, Ga.: Mercer University Press, 1986.
Washington, Joseph R., Jr. *Black Sects and Cults: The Power Axis in the Ethnic Ethic.* Garden City, N. Y.: Doubleday Anchor Books, 1973.
West, Cornel. *Prophetic Fragments.* Grand Rapids: Wm. B. Eerdmans, 1988.
Williams, James D., ed. *The State of Black America.* New York: The National Urban League, Inc., 1986.
Wilmore, Gayraud S., and Cone, James H. *Black Theology: A Documentary History, 1966–1979.* New York: Orbis Books, 1979.
————. *Black Religion and Black Radicalism.* New York: Doubleday & Co., 1973.
Zinn, Howard. *A People's History of the United States.* New York: Harper & Row, 1980.